The ELECTRONIC $ MONEY MACHINE

PROFITS FROM YOUR HOME COMPUTER

The ELECTRONIC $ MONEY MACHINE

PROFITS FROM YOUR HOME COMPUTER

THE · HAVEN · GROUP

AVON
PUBLISHERS OF BARD, CAMELOT, DISCUS AND FLARE BOOKS

THE ELECTRONIC MONEY MACHINE is an original publication of Avon Books. This work has never before appeared in book form.

AVON BOOKS
A division of
The Hearst Corporation
1790 Broadway
New York, New York 10019

Published by arrangement with the authors
Book design by Bob Fitzpatrick
Library of Congress Catalog Card Number: 83-45974
ISBN: 0-380-86751-6

First Avon Printing, March, 1984

Printed in the U. S. A.

DON 10 9 8 7 6 5 4 3 2 1

Notice to Readers

This book is sold with the understanding that neither the authors nor the publisher are engaged in rendering legal, accounting, or money management services. Questions relating to law, accounting, or money management should be addressed to members of those professions.

The authors and publisher specifically disclaim any liability, loss, or risk, personal or otherwise, incurred as a consequence, direct or indirect, of use or application of any contents of this book.

Acknowledgments

The Haven Group thanks all those who gave generously of time, expertise, and general encouragement, especially James M. McGuire, John Wandell, and the staff of the New Haven Public Library, New Haven, Connecticut. Additional appreciation is due to Richard Curtis of the Richard Curtis Agency, and John Douglas, Senior Editor at Avon Books.

We must finally acknowledge the support of our husbands, wives, POSSLQs, cats, and friends, without whom we would have gone nuts long before we finished this book, instead of *just* before. . . .

Contents

List of Trademarks mentioned in this book

Atari™ is a trademark of Atari, Inc.

Apple™, Apple DOS™, Apple IIe™, and AppleWriter™ are trademarks of Apple Computer, Inc.

Boss™ is a trademark of Balcones Computer Corp.

CBASIC™ and CP/M™ are trademarks of Digital Research, Inc.

CompuServe™ is a trademark of CompuServe, Inc.

dBase™ and dBase II™ are trademarks of Ashton-Tate, Inc.

Deadline™ is a trademark of Infocom, Inc.

Electric Pencil™ is a trademark of Michael Shrayer.

Easy Writer™ is a trademark of Information Unlimited Software, Inc.

The Final Word™ is a trademark of Mark of the Unicorn, Inc.

Lotus 1-2-3™ is a trademark of Lotus Development Corp.

Legal Tender™ is a trademark of American CompuSoft.

MicroDecision™ is a trademark of Morrow.

MicroPro™ is a trademark of MicroPro Corp.

Microsoft™ is a trademark of Microsoft Corp.

Multiplan™ is a trademark of Microsoft Corp.

Market Analyzer™, Market Microscope™, and Market Manager™ are trademarks of Dow Jones & Co., Inc.

Perfect Calc™, Perfect Writer™, and Perfect Filer™ are trademarks of Perfect Software, Inc.

The Professional™ is a trademark of American CompuSoft.

SuperCalc™ is a trademark of Sorcim Corp.

The Source™ is a trademark of Source Telecomputing, a subsidiary of Reader's Digest Association, Inc.

Scripsit™ is a trademark of Tandy/Radio Shack.

TRS-8Ø™ and TRSDOS™ are trademarks of Tandy/Radio Shack.

Volkswriter™ is a trademark of Lifetree Software, Inc.

VisiCalc™ is a trademark of VisiCorp., Inc.

WordStar™ is a trademark of MicroPro, Inc.

Xerox™ is a trademark of The Xerox Corporation.

Z-8Ø™ is a trademark of Zilog, Inc.

Zork™ is a trademark of Infocom, Inc.

INTRODUCTION

You Need This Book

At this very moment, you're standing in a bookstore, wishing a little voice would tell you whether or not *The Electronic Money Machine* is a good buy. You've looked at the cover illustration, skimmed the blurbs on the back, and weighed the book in the palm of your hand to get a rough ounces-per-cent feel for it.

What you want, though, is a sense-per-cent feel for it.

So let us try to help you make up your mind. Granted, we're biased—we do have a vested interest in promoting sales of our modest guide to fame and fortune—but we also know who we are, why we wrote this book, and what its contents have done for us.

See, we're not computer science majors. We don't design hardware for IBM or write software for MicroPro. We don't work for ComputerLand or Radio Shack or Atari.

We're five ordinary people—well, as ordinary as freelance writers ever get—who stumbled into the magical realm of the personal computer a couple years back and have been entranced ever since. We love this stuff. And we think you will, too.

But we're not selling computers, we're plugging a book, so let's get right to the question. Do you or do you not need *this* book? Take this short, simple quiz:

Do you hate computers?
Is your last name Rockefeller or Getty?
Does tedium soothe your soul?

If you answered "Yes" to each of the above, stop reading here, put the book back on the rack, and spend your money on *sigh* something else.

If, however, you answered "No" to any of the questions, bear with us a while longer. *The Electronic Money Machine* just might be for you. It probably is, if you fit any of the following descriptions:

Description #1

You're fascinated by computers. You ache to own one, but you haven't bought one. Either you don't have the money, or you can't justify spending a few thousand dollars when you have bills to pay, and the kids' tuition to save for.

Does that fit? Then

Buy *The Electronic Money Machine* because:

A. We'll show you ways to get your system free of charge.
B. We'll explain how to qualify for Uncle Sam's generous discount on your personal computer.
C. We'll detail for you how whatever investment you do make will yield a better return than a CD at your neighborhood bank.

Description #2

You went out and spent half the price of a new car on a system, which didn't bother you because you had the bread, and hey! got to keep up with the times, right? But now you've lost your job, or the insurance didn't cover the flood damage, or the parakeet's vocal coach is demanding a raise, and you sure could use more income—or less outgo.

Is that you? Then

Buy *The Electronic Money Machine* because:

A. We'll show you how your system can save you money.
B. We'll describe its possibilities for managing your finances over both the long and short term.
C. We'll explain the ways in which it can turn you a tidy profit, indeed.

Description #3

Money is absolutely no problem for you, and you don't in any way need either the capital you spent on your system, or the cash flow and tax savings it could generate for you. You do wonder if maybe that sales rep didn't sell you a bill of goods, though. He promised that you'd find it invaluable. But ever since you figured out how to blast all the little Space Invaders, you've only found it dusty. Surely the damn thing must be good for something. You just wish you knew for what.

Is that what's troubling you, Bunky? Then

Buy *The Electronic Money Machine* because:

A. We'll describe some of the ways in which your personal computer can simplify your daily life by reducing if not eliminating some of life's little tedia.
B. We'll talk about the home computer's ability to enrich your intellectual life by extending your range of inquiry.
C. We need your money more than you do.

Our philosophy throughout this book is unabashedly capitalistic. We believe that you're entitled to a return—tangible or otherwise—on your investment.

We believe that in today's America, the cliché "Time is money" has never been more true. If you're an average person, you don't get paid for doing a job—you get paid for the time you spend doing it. Your hours are your unit of investment. By saving yourself time, you save money; by saving other people's time, you make money.

And everyone's better off for it, too.

We believe further that a personal computer is a sizable investment which should—regardless of its main use—pay for itself in the long run.

And finally, we believe that anyone with a modicum of curiosity, a smidgeon of inventiveness, and a dash of perseverance can learn to use a microcomputer to immense personal profit.

So if you fit *that* description, then

You need this book.

Put its advice to work for you. We have. We're here, in this book.

Where would you like to be?

Let us help you get there.

—New Haven, September 1, 1983

PART I

CHAPTER 1

What Else Do You Need?

In addition to this book, you do need a few other things in order to start making and saving money by using your personal computer as the foundation of your Very Small Business—your VSB. But you'll have to make some decisions.

The second thing you'll need to decide is what computer and printer to get.

The *first* thing you'll need to decide is what programs you want your future computer to run, what programs will do the things you will want your computer to do.

That may sound backward, but it isn't. Not all computers can run all programs. You don't want to get yourself a machine that's fine and dandy and able to run everything . . . *except* the one or two programs it *must* run.

In the computer trade, the machines themselves—computers, video screens, disk drives, modems, printers, etc.—are called *hardware,* while the programs are known as *software.* (Then there's *wetware,* the biological devices that manipulate the hardware and software—that's you and me.) While we're not going to use a whole lot of jargon in this book, you should remember the difference between hardware and software.

You'll need both.

You do *not* have to run out and buy one of each of the following kinds of software. It's perfectly possible to start your VSB with just an operating system and one software package, expanding both your services and your income by adding others later, when your budget and your earnings have made that possible.

Software

A casual glance at the ads in a recent issue of any computer magazine reveals that literally thousands of different software packages are available—so many, in fact, that it's easy to get confused.

No problem. All software packages fall into one of the following categories:

Operating systems are the master programs, the ones that tell your computer how to work: what each keystroke means, where and how to write a file, or how to print. These tend to be tied closely to a given machine. If you have a CP/M™ machine, it probably won't be able to use the UCSD p-system without major surgery.

While there are many fine operating systems around, the most common are CP/M and MS-DOS. We recommend that you get a computer that can operate on one or both of these, simply because they are so common, and there are so many programs and packages that each can run. Most of the time, you won't have to buy the CP/M operating system separately; it'll come with the machine.

Some machines—the Apple and the TRS-8Ø are two examples—have their own operating systems, designed by the manufacturer specifically for the computer. In many cases, these computers can be equipped to run CP/M. But that takes extra money and effort; getting a machine that is already comfortable with either CP/M or MS-DOS saves you trouble.

Text editors are the programs that turn a computer into a *very* intelligent and flexible typewriter. With a text editor, you can juggle blocks of words; correct errors simply; write letters, articles, and books; and generally do anything you could do with a typewriter—only faster and better.

There are many, many different text editors (also known as word-processing packages) available on the market, with names like AppleWriter™, Electric Pencil™, Select™, Volkswriter™, and The Final Word™. One of the most popular is MicroPro's WordStar™; in fact, it comes free with several machines. An advantage to choosing that one as your text editor is that, once you know how to use it, you can make money teaching other people how to use it. Many law offices, for example, are buying WordStar-equipped computers, and are willing to pay upwards of $2ØØ per day for instruction.

When shopping for a text editor, give flexibility a higher priority than initial ease of use. Linked to the proper printer, your text editor should be able to produce micro-justified copy, so that you can do things like prepare camera-ready copy for books and pamphlets; it should also be able to handle a wide variety of formats.

Any text editor, though, will let you run a super-typing business, allowing you to promise your customers error-free copy and cheap revisions. When you make changes in a letter, article, or thesis with a text editor, you don't have to retype the parts of it that are right. You only correct the errors and insert changes.

Spreadsheets with names like SuperCalc™, VisiCalc™, and Perfect Calc™, are wonderful. With them, and without any programming background, you can create programs to balance checkbooks, predict sales, do small payrolls, and estimate costs. They can even help you with your taxes. And all of the calculations are handled by the machine. (See Chapter 11 for more on the VSB use of spreadsheets.)

While spreadsheets are great for calculations and projections, as file clerks they are awkward. For record keeping—your clients' and your own— you can get more productivity out of

Database management systems (DBMS) like Minimum Data Base™, dBase II™, and Perfect Filer™. A DBMS is an even more sophisticated—and effective—tool for keeping and handling records. Their only drawbacks are that they are difficult to learn and expensive to buy. (As usual, every cloud has a silver lining. Once you've learned how to use a DBMS, others will pay you to teach them.) But for handling large quantities of data—invoices, billing records, large payrolls, etc.—they can't be beat.

Communications packages work together with a modem (see below). They let your computer hook up, via your telephone lines, with other computers or teletext services, giving you access to large libraries of free programs and even to wire services. While getting into communications can be fun, these are clearly optional packages.

Languages for programming, like BASIC, FORTRAN, COBOL, PASCAL and MODULA II, allow you to create your own programs to do anything within the limits of your computer's capabilities and your skills.

However, unless you know programming already, it will take a lot of time and effort to learn how to do it well. Until you've put in that time and effort, you'll be competing in the programming world under a huge handicap.

That's the bad news. The good news is that the variety of available prepackaged programs nearly guarantees that there is a program out there that will do what you want one to do. It may be available free (there are a lot of free programs around) or at a price—but it will almost certainly be available.

Unless you're already a programmer, we suggest that you leave programming alone, at least at first. There are many, many other ways to make a few dollars. Or more than a few.

Utilities are programs written in machine language. They do things like prepare disks for use, copy files from one disk to another, tell you how much space you have left on a disk, or keep lists of the files you have on your collection of disks. You'll need quite a few of these, but most will come with your operating system. Many others are in the public domain and are available, on disks that your machine can read, from mail-order suppliers at low cost. CP/M users can get scads of inexpensive utilities and other programs from the CP/M User's Group (see **Appendix**).

Essential Hardware

If you already have your complete system, you can skip this section and move on to the next; if not, let's go shopping.

As a VSB operator, you must have the following pieces of hardware. We'll get to the options later.

The microprocessor is the heart of the computer. This is the little electronic chip that actually does all of the calculation. It is often hidden inside one of the other pieces of equipment. The Xerox 82Ø, for example, keeps its microprocessor inside its video display; the Radio Shack Model I's microprocessor is hidden inside the keyboard; the Cromemco System 1's is tucked into its disk drive enclosure.

No matter; unless you're into computer repair or the more exotic branches of programming, you don't have to know where your microprocessor is, or even how it does what it does. You do have to know two things:

1. Some microprocessors work faster than others. An example: One popular chip is the Z8Ø; its cousin, a different chip called the Z8ØA, is 6Ø percent faster. Price considerations being equal, faster is better.

However, it's important to remember that the speed of your computer doesn't depend only on the speed of the chip. Even the fastest chip in the world won't drive a 1Ø-character-per-second printer at 2Ø characters per second; and even the quickest disk drives usually run *much* slower than the slowest microprocessor.

The proper way to compare is side by side. Have the sales rep set up two different machines to do the same thing, and see.

2. Some microprocessors can control more memory than others. Without a whole lot of software trickery, 8-bit machines can talk directly to (''address'' is the jargon) just about 64,ØØØ bytes (think of a byte as an individual letter or number) of memory; 16-bit machines can address more than a million bytes. When using, for example, a word-processing package, most of an 8-bit computer's memory will be taken up by the word-processing program, leaving little space for the text itself.

That makes the 16-bit machines seem much better than the 8-bit ones. A program that takes up 48,000 bytes (48K), would leave an 8-bit machine only 16,000 bytes to hold whatever you're writing—about 2500 words, or ten double-spaced typewriter pages.

Fortunately, while that's true, it's incomplete. The better word-processing programs will automatically write your text onto a disk as you work. You'll never notice that the computer is actually handling only a small part of what you're writing at any given time.

The main advantage of the 16-bit machines over the 8-bit ones is that they are faster; their main disadvantage is that they tend to be more expensive.

Again, the only proper comparison is head-to-head.

Disk drives come in three main types. While you can mix and match to a certain extent, you will need at least two drives, no matter what the sales rep says. (One who tells you otherwise is either ignorant, or trying to represent the machine as less expensive than it really is. If you buy just one drive, you will have to come back [not to *that* store] and get another.) The reason that you need two is that you will often have to copy disks and transfer files. You need at least two drives—one to copy from; the other to copy to—in order to do that.

Floppy disk drives aren't really flimsy: the *disks* are flexible. Their *raison d'être* is that the disks can be removed; this lets you store your programs and files safely when you turn off the machine. Although they come in a variety of formats and sizes, the main distinction is how much information each disk will hold. That ranges from about 80,000 bytes of information—less than one-tenth of this book—all the way to 1,500,000 bytes—more than twice the length of this book. While the more memory you have, the better, even the least capacious drives are acceptable for the beginning VSB operator.

Floppy drives are slower and less expensive than the other kinds of drives. Handle all floppy disks very carefully;

if you ever touch a finger to the disk itself, you can kiss it goodbye.

Most software comes on floppy disks; you will need at least one of these drives to be able to use packaged programs. Unless you can get a good deal on a hard disk or a pseudodisk, you will need two floppy drives.

Hard disk drives are also known as Winchester drives. These store much more data than floppies—up to 2Ø million bytes, the equivalent of twenty-five to thirty full-length novels.

They are spacious, and anywhere from two to five times as fast as floppy drives, but much more expensive. Many have "nonremovable media," which means that the disk is permanently implanted in the disk drive. No changing disks; if you run out of space, you'll have to clear some room by erasing. Some of the newer ones have "removable media," which allow you to pull out an old disk and pop in a new one.

Pseudodisks or disk emulators aren't really disks at all. A disk emulator is a bunch of Random Access Memory (RAM) chips, just like your computer's main memory, that have been tricked into thinking they are a disk.

These phoneys are the speediest there are; they'll let you run programs much faster than even the fastest hard disk. The disadvantage is that they're volatile: when the machine is turned off—or the power fails—everything in their memory goes to never-never land. But for working with, they can't be beat: you work with the pseudodisk, then transfer what you've done over to a floppy.

The best news about pseudodisks is that their prices are continuing to fall. As of this writing, a particular one-megabyte pseudodisk is available for $1ØØØ as a special promotion; that could easily be the standard price within just a few years.

A nonoption that some sales reps will try to sell you is a cassette tape recorder instead of disk drives. Cassettes have one advantage: they are much cheaper than real disk drives.

They have only two disadvantages: they are incredibly slow, and even more unreliable. You don't want to lose valuable data to the vagaries of a cassette tape recorder. Use a tape recorder to play music while you work; *don't* use it to store your programs and files.

The terminal consists of a keyboard and a cathode ray tube (CRT) monitor. These are the most noticeable parts of the computer, and the parts you'll be dealing with directly all of the time. Make sure that you like both.

You should be able to read words on the CRT without eyestrain. Letters should be large enough and sharp enough to be easily legible. Some CRTs show white letters on a black background; some use green letters; others display orange; some even can display black on white, just like a page of printing. It's all a matter of personal preference. Unless you're unusually subject to eyestrain, any good CRT will do.

What isn't optional is the range of the CRT. The industry assumes a "full line" to be at least 80 characters wide, but some screens, like the Osborne 1's, for example, don't show a full line. Upgrade kits are available to let you see the full screen, but be certain to include the cost of the upgrade in your cost calculations. You will need a full-screen CRT, no matter what you're doing.

Keyboards are a problem. As of this writing, no computer keyboard has a really nice feel. Some manufacturers try to compensate by building in a keyclick, or a simulation of a typewriter's tactile feedback, but you'll have to live with something not as good as an electric typewriter's feel.

Some machines do feel nicer than others. Try a few.

Another big difference between keyboards is the presence or absence of programmable function keys. These keys can group several keystrokes together, making your keyboard easier and faster to use. They're very handy, and should be considered a plus.

An essential feature is one you can't see. It's called "N-key rollover." This feature prevents you from issuing an undesired command when you accidentally hit more than three keys at the same time.

Which you will. Be certain that your keyboard has N-key rollover. If it does, it will be mentioned on the specifications sheet that the sales rep will show you. (It might also be called a "keyboard buffer.")

Getting it all together is the next step. After all that talk about the different parts of the system, you may be tempted to get your entire computer as part of a package—perhaps all in one unit, like the Osborne 1 or KayPro II.

You should be. Generally, buying a package can save you quite a bit of money over buying your terminal, disks, and microprocessor unit separately. Further, many packages come complete with software—up to several thousand dollars' worth.

On top of that, by buying from one manufacturer, you increase the ease of getting repairs, while generally decreasing the cost of your service contract (see below).

So consider it, but do make your judgment based on the characteristics we've discussed here. No matter how good the price, if your new machine can't do what you want it to, you won't be happy with it.

Printers

Choosing a printer causes much expense and agony for beginning computer users. Printers appropriate for a personal-computer owner come in two basic types: dot-matrix, and daisywheel. Dot-matrix printers have three main advantages over daisywheel ones: (1) they are generally faster than daisywheel printers—4Ø characters per second is considered snappy for a daisywheel while slow for a dot-matrix; (2) many of them can do graphs and charts quite nicely; and (3) they are much less expensive. A good dot-matrix printer may cost about $7ØØ; a good daisywheel printer will run more than $12ØØ.

They have only one disadvantage, and that one is critical. The printing of most dot-matrix printers looks like this:

Not very good, eh? This looks
like it was printed by a computer,
as indeed it was. For work where it
is important that the text look
good, this is clearly unsuitable.
If you only have a dot-matrix
printer, you won't get any business
typing term papers and theses, doing
form letter mailings for local

businesses, or Christmas letters for neighbors, or anything of that sort. While the best dot-matrix printers can produce what is called Near Letter Quality (NLQ) copy, their work still looks like computer-generated text.

Daisywheel printing, on the other hand, looks like this; many different typefaces are available. It's perfectly suitable for form letters and theses; indeed, this sort of printing is fine for anything short of camera-ready copy for books and the like, where the customer wants the copy to look like it was printed on a press.

Some daisywheel printers and word-processing packages can do this -- proportional space printing. In this sort of printing, the computer and printer understand that each letter has a different width. With a daisywheel printer and a proportional space wheel, you can prepare camera-ready copy for books, or letterheads, or anything where the ultimate in appearance is necessary.

A daisywheel printer ranges in price from about $500 to more than $2000. Generally, you get what you pay for; the more expensive machines print faster, and tend to break down less often.

That last is important. On the specifications sheet, look for a figure usually called Mean Time Between Failures or MTBF. This is the average number of hours you'll be able to use your printer between calls to the service technician. A simple way to find out how highly your sales rep rates a given printer is to ask the cost of a service contract on the machine. The less the contract costs, the more certain the store is that the machine won't need frequent trips to the shop. (See **The Service Contract** below.)

Printer alternatives are possible if you already have a typewriter. If you have an electronic typewriter, it may be possible to equip it with an interface so your computer can use it as a printer. There are devices on the market that clip onto a typewriter's keyboard, and, in effect, use mechanical fingers to type as your computer commands. As always, you can't make a judgment until you actually see the device in action. Don't be too shy to politely ask the salesman to show you a working demo model before you write a check.

Optional Hardware

Modems are devices that let your computer talk over the phone. With a modem and a communications package, you can exchange programs with other users, or tie into The Source™ or CompuServe™ services. Those will give you access to even more programs and games, plus wire service and newspaper stories.

We suggest that you start without a modem; there will be time enough to get into communications later on.

Plotters can give you better graphics capability than even the best dot-matrix printers. That can be essential if your VSB involves preparing attractive charts and graphs. Their disadvantage is that they are comparable in price to daisywheel printers.

Uninterruptible power sources (UPS) can protect your data if your power shuts off. Basically, they are batteries and electronic circuits that, for a short period of time, substitute for your house current in the event of a power loss, allowing you a few minutes to close your files and shut down your machine.

Surge protectors are for just the opposite problem. If your house current spikes erratically, it may harm your machine. A surge protector allows only the proper amount of juice to flow into your computer. Some machines have surge protection built in. Check the spec sheets.

Printer buffers may be a big help if you want to use

your computer for something else while it's printing. The gizmos hook up between your computer and printer. In effect, the computer "prints" into the buffer, then lets you go your merry way with whatever you're doing while your printer churns out the copy.

Some machines are already able to print and do other work at the same time; they don't need buffers.

Essential Middleware: The Service Contract

You have to have one. You really do. While microcomputers are becoming more sophisticated and reliable, they do break down. Unless you are *very* sure of what you're doing, you can't repair it yourself. You'll have to call the repairman. (If you really *do* know enough to repair your own machine, see Chapter 10, "Big Bucks in a Tool Kit." If you're good enough to fix yours, you're good enough to fix theirs.)

If you don't have a service contract with your repairman, his time clock starts ticking the moment he gets to your door (or, in some cases, sooner), at upwards of $50 an hour. You'll sweat as he spends twenty-seven cents of your money just turning your machine on; or takes out a moment to light up a cigarette, charging you fifty cents for the time he spends doing it; or sits down for twelve minutes—$10—to figure out where the glitch is.

On the other hand, if you have a service contract, the time problem is on the other side: You've already paid for all of the service your machine will need, and your serviceman will want to finish the repairs just as quickly as possible.

The flaw with these yearly service contracts (AKA "yearly maintenance agreements") is that they are expensive. They tend to run 10 percent to 15 percent of the retail price of the equipment. Shop around a bit; even within one area, the price of a service contract on the same machine may vary. And do check with other customers before signing one; you want to be sure that the serviceman really does zip right out to fix things.

Service contracts are essential. Without one, a single

blown resistor can easily run you 25 percent or more of the cost of your equipment.

If you already own a computer, you might want to skip to Chapter 3. Otherwise,

TURN THE PAGE.

CHAPTER 2

How to Get a Computer Even Though You Can't Afford It

There are many advantages to buying big-ticket items cheaply. For the budding entrepreneur, access to inexpensive or free hardware, software, and supplies can transform a marginal operation into a money-maker, or breathe life into an otherwise foredoomed effort.

Many people who start home businesses with microcomputers begin, not surprisingly, with an interest in microcomputers. They can cite specifications, availability of software and peripherals, list prices, and dealers' markups. When the idea for a Very Small Business presents itself, they know just where to go for the most economical equipment, best suited to the profession they've chosen for themselves.

If they succeed in that profession, however, it will be through sheer good luck. They know what the business needs from them, but they've neglected to consider what they need from the business. Disappointment, confusion, and financial hardship can be the result.

Affordable Is What YOU Can Afford

Millions of people make money from the computer industry every day. Only a few of those people are in business for themselves, and a like fraction are making a living wage. The spectrum of computer capitalists runs from the weekend hacker who sells cassette versions of home-cooked utility programs, to the MIT graduates who founded Infocom and are now responsible for two of 1983's five best-selling games, *Zork I*™ and *Deadline*™.

Where do you fit on the spectrum? You may want your VSB to put you through school, buy you a few luxuries, or help you to achieve financial independence or to command great wealth . . . or you may simply want to justify the expense of a computer system you would have bought anyway.

Whatever your purpose, you need to decide how much you will invest in your VSB. You need to know how much, if any, of your investment you can afford to lose. And you must tailor your VSB to your own financial situation.

For example, we know a university professor who became interested in computers as a hobby. He was able to invest about $6000 in an Apple III, a printer, programs, and supplies without pinching the family budget too much. At first he used the system to organize his home finances and generate form letters sent to students applying to the graduate study program in his department. Soon after, he became interested in programming and wrote a program to calculate salary increases for his department's faculty—a complicated procedure which, using a calculator, took about a half hour for each of several dozen individuals.

Realizing his talent and seeing a market for it, he invested a smaller amount in a business phone and answering machine at his home, a pamphlet, and some advertising, and set himself up as a designer of custom software. Last we heard, he had recouped the second, smaller investment, and was on his way to "paying back" the first $6000 as well—money which, at first, he had considered the cost of a hobby.

His case is quite different from that of a woman we know who, after fifteen years of a 9-to-5 existence, decided she wanted to be her own boss. She saw her VSB as a way to financial independence. She also spent about $6000, but thanks to careful shopping her money went farther. Using borrowed money to purchase a Xerox 820-II computer with eight-inch disk drives, a Diablo 630 letter-quality printer, the WordStar word-processing program, and sundry supplies, she set herself up as a one-woman word-processing business serving a large, local contingent of graduate students.

Even though she had put aside enough savings during those fifteen long years to live for one or even two years without discomfort, she had to start making a good wage from her system at once—to make the payments on the system and service contract, and to ensure that she would never have to return to a workaday job.

Both entrepreneurs spent about the same amount on their systems, and both knew their markets and capabilities before they set themselves up in business. For the university professor, an unsuccessful venture would have meant fewer luxuries and perhaps some embarrassment. For the word-processing businesswoman, anything but a strong showing would have meant financial disaster—perhaps a crippling one.

Both, at last report, were doing well.

What you can afford to lose is your first consideration.

What you can expect to make is your second.

Typing and word processing command a fairly steady market, since they deal with a large pool of people who have similar needs. Writing custom programs is not a steady market, even though the "hourly wage" is likely to be higher.

Considering her financial situation, the businesswoman would have met disaster if she had tried to set herself up in the custom software business. Conversely, constraints on the professor's time would have made the word-processing business a disaster for him. It wouldn't have been much fun for him, either, and fun was one of the primary "profits" from *his* VSB.

When considering the financial situation of your VSB,

1. **Remember the 50 percent rule.** It applies to everything. A job will take 50 percent longer to finish than you expect. Your costs will be 50 percent higher than you estimate. Your income will be 50 percent less than you consider reasonable.

No matter how carefully you calculate your estimated income and expenses in advance, the 50 percent rule will apply. Figure it in. After you have been in business for a while, you can safely reduce this "fudge factor"—unless, of course, you find that you must increase it.

2. **Leave yourself a fallback.** If your business is unsuccessful, or you lose interest, can you (and will you want to) sell your equipment and supplies? If not, will they add an unaffordable expense to your budget?

The way to narrow the gap between the amount you need to spend and the amount you expect to make is to:

3. **Reduce start-up costs.** The average markup on hardware, from manufacturer to individual purchaser, is 40 percent. The markup on software is a staggering 50 percent. Since hardware and software are your biggest expenses, the more you can cut your retailer's profit margin, the better your chances for starting and maintaining a successful home business.

Cutting your initial costs by 25—or even 5—percent may make the difference between your starting now, a year from now, or not at all.

And *failing* to cut expenses costs you more than the extra expense. If you start your VSB with borrowed money and fail to save $1000, it costs you $1000 *plus interest.* If you start with money you've earned at a job, and you are in the 20-percent tax bracket, failing to save $1000 may cost you *$1200.* (Unless, of course, taking a loss is to your advantage, taxwise. See chapter 12, "Deep in the Heart of Taxes.")

Whether you are buying cans of tuna fish or personal computers, the first, best, and easiest way to make money is to save money.

A Penny Saved Is a Penny You Earned

We said it was easy. We didn't say it was effortless. It takes work and skill to find the best buys in hardware, software, and supplies. But once you've found them, you'll use more time and skill to take advantage of those buys.

Buying by mail takes careful research. Any large purchase represents a risk, and a large mail-order purchase is a particularly large risk. A bad disk can be muttered over, then discarded without hardship. A microcomputer whose cracked processor board transforms it into an odd, unwieldy paperweight can be brought back to the retailer—if you bought it at a retailer.

If you bought it by mail, however, you have no sales rep to berate or charm into giving you a new one. You have an address or toll-free number, an anonymous typewriter or inflectionless voice—and your familiar mailman or UPS deliveryman, who may bring you a worthwhile purchase, a first-rate disaster, or, after many hopeful weeks, nothing at all.

On the other hand, if you know what you're doing, your common sense and careful research may bring you discounts of about 2Ø percent on hardware, more on software and supplies.

When buying hardware by mail, stick with brands serviced by manufacturers' own regional service centers or by third-party service organizations. Xerox Service Centers, located in thirty-six states as of this writing, offer walk-in service not only for their own products but for Osborne, Morrow, and Corona, and for peripherals by Amdek, Epson, and Diablo.

TeleVideo's fine line of computers is not as widely available as some others, and several mail-order houses specialize in this line. Since TeleVideo storefront retailers are few, and since the stores don't service the line anyway (TRW's regional offices do), you don't lose much dealer support if you buy this brand by mail.

Do be careful, when mail-ordering equipment, not to

get ripped off or caught in someone else's financial difficulties. Infamous now is the case of the mail-order house offering generous discounts on a full line of microcomputers and peripherals. Located in Texas, the company shipped orders overnight to local customers, and was somewhat slower in shipping to customers in neighboring states.

If you happened to live far beyond the borders of Texas, the company simply kept your money.

Shipping locally avoided problems with state and local consumer offices and law enforcement agencies. More distant customers had little recourse but to file complaints with the U.S. Postal Service or the Texas or federal attorneys general. The business was eventually shut down and the operators indicted, but in the meantime hundreds of customers lost thousands of dollars.

Less nefarious but equally disastrous is the newly founded mail-order house that goes bankrupt after it receives your order but before your order is shipped.

You can eliminate the risk of getting nothing for your money by buying COD. This will cost you in the neighborhood of 3 percent over your discounted purchase price. You have a check or large wad of cash ready for the postman when he arrives with your goods. While he probably won't wait on the porch for the several hours or days you'll take to get your system up and running, you will at least have the opportunity to reject visibly damaged, unsealed, or otherwise suspicious-looking cartons before you hand over any payment.

If a mail-order company will not ship goods COD, don't deal with them unless you have more venturesome friends who have already dealt with the company and received satisfaction—and even then, keep your purchases small.

Nearly all mail-order houses offer the convenience of accepting MasterCard, Visa, and other credit cards. Be aware that charges are usually made against your account the day your order is received, not the day it is sent—which may be days or weeks later.

Don't send a money order. All you get from the post office or bank is a receipt proving that you purchased a money order in a certain amount. The bank or post office, not you, receives the proof that the money order was cashed. This proof can take considerable time to track down, in the event that problems develop with your order.

If you send a check, mail-order houses will wait up to two weeks for it to clear before they ship your merchandise, which may be inconvenient for you. But when your bank statement arrives you will at least have proof that they did receive money from you.

If you don't have friends who have dealt with the mail-order house whose offers are most attractive, apply the two-year test. Since you probably became interested in the mail-order company through its advertisements in computer magazines, refer to a two-year-old issue of the magazine and see if the company has been in business over that span of time. Two years is usually enough time for law enforcement agencies to sniff out blatant scams. A company that has gotten through two or more years as an advertiser in a major magazine is probably legitimate and on a sound financial footing.

While buying hardware and peripherals by mail is risky and requires special care, mail order is the ideal way to purchase software. You can seldom try out any but the largest-selling programs in a store. And since you've read the same reviews of the software as the retailer or sales rep has, you probably know as much about it as they do.

Most software publishers maintain a hot line you can call or an address to write to if you have problems with a software package; this is another service the retailer is unable to offer. And updates of the program, available to purchasers of the previous version, come only from the publisher.

So, for software, mail order is the way to go. You will need to educate yourself before you send away for the stuff, but you would have had to do that anyway. To buy software from any source, you will need to be able to read a software description. In particular, you will need to know

1. whether the software will run on your computer's operating system;
2. whether your printer and disk drives will support it;
3. how much memory it requires;
4. what it does and what its limitations are;

5. what documentation is available;
6. whether or not you can modify it yourself; and
7. what language it is written in.

This information is generally contained in the mail-order catalogue's software description. You'll also need to know whether the software requires additional packages to run, whether it can interface with others, and what kind of disk storage it requires for data.

The other cheap way to get software is to pirate it for yourself. This method gives you a 100 percent discount. It's also known as a "five-finger discount"—because it is stealing.

Pirating software is illegal, although there's little chance of your getting caught if you don't sell copies. It is immoral, too, and is one reason for the rising price of software. Publishers are trying to make money not only on you, but on the folks to whom you're giving the copyrighted programs. As the number of households with home computers rises, the piracy problem is going to balloon, sending markups on software even higher.

Supplies like disks, printer ribbons, and paper should be bought by mail whenever possible. You can't get and probably don't need much dealer support for these. Buy small quantities of the products by mail until you find the brands you prefer. Then buy larger quantities at larger discounts, to save more money and ensure that you are never caught without a blank disk.

For more on mail-order buying, see Chapter 8, "You Can Get It for Them Wholesale."

Getting Stuff Free

Sometimes retailers and manufacturers will *give* you things! Here's why:

Computers are seldom sold to retailers on a consignment basis. Rather, the wholesaler or manufacturer requires cash up front for each of the several dozen machines it takes to stock even a small computer store. Computer retailers naturally turn to banks for some of their start-up costs; thus, a machine that retails at $3000 and wholesales for $2400 may cost the retailer $57 per month for five years.

What can you do that the retailer will think is worth $57 per month?

If you know how, you can teach the retailer's customers how to use their new computers. Of course, you ought to *have* a computer like those the retailer is selling. Perhaps you could make a trade: your time and expertise for the retailer's computer and software packs.

You might offer promotion, too. We know a businessman who bought a relatively inexpensive Apple II from a dealer several years ago, and became a regular customer of the Apple retailer. The retailer later expanded his line to include Victor computers. At that time, Victor was known and respected in Europe but little known in the United States.

Victor extended generous discounts to its dealers to encourage them to take on the machine, and the retailer swapped a Victor 9000 and accessories, plus a complete line of software, in exchange for word-of-mouth promotion and the businessman's agreement to (1) use the Victor to write a report for a sales convention, and (2) acknowledge the Victor 9000's contribution to his presentation to the several hundred business people in attendance at the convention.

After the convention, the businessman had the option of returning the 9000—or buying it for 80 percent off list price!

Any of the skills you can use to start a VSB can also be bartered for hardware. But because proficiency with computers is nearly always required before you can make this kind of deal, this strategy works best for those who already have access to computers (at work or school), or for those who have systems and want to expand or upgrade them.

Build It Yourself

The cost of the parts in the average $3000 system is only a few hundred dollars. All the rest is assembly and overhead cost. Building a system from blank epoxy boards and several hundred chips is not recommended, even for those with the skill to do it. The investment in tools, instruments, and time is prohibitive—as is the fact that your home-built system will probably have trouble interacting with commercially available peripherals.

You can save $1000 on the Zenith Z-89 microcomputer by buying it as the Heath H-89 and assembling it yourself.

The Heath/Zenith is the only micro widely available in kit form. It uses the CP/M operating systems, and comes with two Z-80 microprocessors and a disk drive. It has an 80-character keyboard and a full-size screen with twenty-four 80-character lines. For $1895, you get all this in component form, with plenty of directions and some tools.

For the same price, however, you can get a KayPro II, Morrow MicroDecision™, Osborne I, or any of several other computers—assembled and with software.

You can save money with the Heath/Zenith kit, but it is recommended more for those who want to learn about computers. After all, it takes time to build a computer, and time is—you guessed it—money.

Printers

You will certainly need a printer for your system, and you may need a letter-quality printer. That doesn't necessarily mean you have to buy one.

Several companies sell devices that plug into the logic boards of IBM's series of electronic typewriters and make the machine responsive to commands fed to it through your computer's RS-232C port. California Micro Computer charges about $400 for theirs, and they say use of it does not void the service contract on your typewriter. (Of course, you can make sure of this by unplugging the device before the service technician arrives.) Output is slow, but if you already own an IBM Electronic 50 typewriter (since discontinued, but retailing for $1400 in 1981, when we bought ours), you will be glad to save the investment you made in your typewriter. And installation of the interface does not prevent you from using your typewriter *as* a typewriter.

You can also get a typewriter with the computer interface already installed. The Olivetti Praxis Bytewriter operates from a Centronics-type port, which may or may not be a problem for your computer. The Bytewriter uses a daisywheel typing element, which is quieter and, all other factors being equal, more reliable than the IBM "golfball" typing element. Price for the Bytewriter is $695—much less than most letter-quality printers.

Which is to say, you don't have to buy what you see in the pretty advertisements. If you don't need a Diablo 63Ø printer, why pay for one?

You don't have to buy new equipment either.

Some People Have More Computers Than They Know What to Do With

The classified ads of your local newspaper often list used computers for sale. The prices are often very attractive, because the present owner is trying to cut a loss. You may find a scarcely used item offered by a business that has outgrown its old system. Would-be hobbyists who find computers not to their taste are sources of used equipment, too.

Buy it only if you can take the item to a service technician who can check out the machine. If you want a service contract on the equipment (and you do), you will have to do this anyway.

Computer-store owners may help you locate used equipment. If they have a prospective customer who is hesitating at the thought of losing the investment he made on his first machine, the retailer will be delighted to bring you together with the prospect. The prospect sells to you; then, the retailer sells to the prospect.

People who work for computer companies are either the best or the worst people from whom to buy equipment. Some companies have employee discount programs, but discourage employees from becoming retailers at the expense of the company's generosity.

On the other hand, we know one VSB operator who got a very nice system as part of an incentive plan. Since the plan was available to his company's sales reps nationwide, there was a brief, small flood of heavily discounted systems on the market. The cost to the company was minimal—the model involved was discontinued soon after—but our friend parlayed that incentive plan with admirable skill.

He used the small system to start his VSB, used the profits from that to buy a larger system for himself, and *rented* the original, small computer to a friend who started his *own* VSB.

The first VSB operator got a small cash flow and a tax break (not to mention his new system), and the second got a machine at nominal charge, enabling him to start his VSB much earlier than would otherwise have been possible.

Here we must mention that, ordinarily, renting is not the way to get your computer system. In fact, unless you find a very special deal, such as you might get from a friend, renting is a sure way to doom your VSB right from the start. It imposes a large and continuing overhead cost, one which will never end until you bite the bullet and buy a computer.

Lanier, A.B. Dick, Wang, and other makers of dedicated word processors *will* rent systems to you—at a cost of about $36Ø per month or more.

If you can afford $36Ø per month, save it and buy a computer.

Leasing may be a bearable compromise. Some of the better-established dealers make arrangements with leasing companies to help customers buy machines with someone else's money. A retailer may send you to a local bank, and the bank will send you a leasing application, including a "net worth" statement for your company.

If you are just starting out, you will have an uphill battle convincing the bank to accept your lease application. Unless you are obviously insolvent, however, you do stand some chance, because the more leases the bank has out, the more money the bank earns—assuming the customers don't default.

For example, you may be able to lease $3ØØØ in hardware for four years, at a cost of $9Ø.3Ø per month including state tax. Add to this the cost of the service contract: about $6ØØ more per year. At the end of the lease you can buy the hardware (because you've already paid for it!) for a small sum—perhaps one dollar.

Banks do not want to make lease agreements for amounts less than several thousand dollars, by the way.

Leasing is not the way to get a few hundred dollars' worth of peripherals and supplies.

Using the Bank's Computer

Borrowing all or part of the start-up costs of your VSB has several advantages. Any interest charges can be deducted on your income tax, as can the cost of all your hardware, software, and supplies. Add your tax credits to these deductions, and the federal government ends up subsidizing your interest costs and a little more.

The disadvantage is the baggage you will be carrying if your VSB is not as profitable as you had hoped. If, after a year, you realize that running your own business is not all it was cracked up to be, you may still have two years' worth of loan to pay off. Your hardware will probably have depreciated faster than the principal of your loan, which means that even if you sell the hardware you will have to dip into savings or current income to pay off the debt. After you have already suffered the shock of failing at your VSB, the obligation to pay old debts will only add to your disappointment.

If your VSB is to be part-time work, and your full-time employer sponsors a credit union, your burden can be eased by lower interest rates. At this writing, commercial banks' personal loan rates hover around 18 percent, while credit unions lend money at 12 to 15 percent.

If you do borrow money, assure the loan officer that your ability to meet your monthly payments will not depend on the success of your business. Apply for a personal loan, not a business loan.

Other Money

Some credit cards offer substantial credit lines to good customers. The MasterCard "gold card," for example, has a $5000 limit, all of which can be gotten in cash if your local computer store doesn't take MasterCard. More modest lines of credit will still enable you to buy peripherals and supplies, while you pay for the computer itself with cash or a bank loan. Keep in mind that credit card interest rates go up to 19½ percent, though, and if you receive a cash advance you may be required to pay a one-time service or handling charge of 3 to 5 percent.

When you have made even one payment toward your credit card debt, you can turn around and charge against it again. This should be done only as a temporary measure, however, since by doing it you are continually paying interest but never reducing your principal debt.

You can borrow against a straight life insurance policy, too. What you are borrowing is a portion of the premiums you have paid over the years. A friend of ours started his VSB by borrowing against his policy and then defaulting on the "loan" of his own money.

Warning! Warning!

Before you start your VSB with money you don't have, recheck the calculations you made on the profitability of the business. Have a friend (whose view of your abilities may be more realistic than your own) go over your calculations with you. The *only* time you can borrow with anything approaching complete confidence is when you are already running a profitable business that would clearly benefit by automation.

While borrowing money may not be a good idea, borrowing time is a lot less risky.

Make Money on Borrowed Time

Nearly all colleges and universities have a large, mainframe computer which is used for student and faculty records, payroll, and by students and faculty to accomplish their research and assignments.

At the beginning of each budget year, departments are assigned a dollar-amount of computer time. The number is not arbitrary, but it is even more fictitious than the amount of the national debt. Department heads assign their faculty a budget, and students apply to faculty for time on the mainframe.

We know one student who, for two years, ran a typing and term paper service on the university's mainframe, enabling him to put himself through school. A sympathetic professor gave him the time he needed, but as the student puts it, "There's always a swindle you can work." If you have any legitimate use for the computer, you can come up with a way to increase your allowed time on it.

The mainframe will be faster, more powerful, and have more storage space than any microcomputer you can buy. All the programs you could want will already be stored on it.

Unfortunately, you do not have complete control over the mainframe, as you would over your personal computer. Files and programs can be lost or inadvertently destroyed, so you will need to make electronic and paper copies of all your work. Also, you will probably not have as much access to the computer as you would like, or at the most convenient times.

Once your VSB starts making a profit, however, you can buy a smart terminal and a modem and dial into the mainframe from your apartment or dormitory room.

On a related note, several universities sponsor large discounts on selected models. At Boston University, for example, even part-time students can buy IBM and Digital personal computers at a 25 percent discount. If you are planning on attending college, or contemplating a transfer, inquire into discounts and access to the mainframe—and consider that a part of the college's financial aid package before you make your decision on which college to attend.

The Art of Negotiation

There is much to be said for buying a computer in the "traditional" manner, through a storefront retail outlet. Many of them service the models they sell. ComputerLand is one of these; in addition, ComputerLand sells only products with a proven track record, eliminating a big source of complications for you and for themselves.

While many salesmen know a lot about selling and virtually nothing about computers, you can usually find at least one sales rep in a large store who has a genuine love for computers and will help you make a wise decision on your purchase. If you can find such a person, the higher retail markup you will pay will be worthwhile—once you have reduced that markup by negotiation. The goal is a good savings for you and a reasonable, not exorbitant, profit for the retailer.

Just knowing you *can* negotiate gives you an advantage over other customers, who think buying computers is like buying canned fruit. The price on the sticker is not *the* price; it is the manufacturer's suggested list price. It is open to dickering. If the sales rep says that it is not, find another sales rep.

Do not expect more than nominal discounts on the various computers that already have a low sticker price and usually offer loads of software as part of the package: Osborne, KayPro II, and Morrow MicroDecision. One reason the prices for these systems are so low is that the manufacturers' or dealers' profits have been reduced already.

Exceptions are models that are discontinued, will be discontinued, or are staying on the market with newer, more capable machines. Osborne 1's, which originally sold for $1795, now go for $900 or less, since Osborne went bankrupt. The KayPro II, offered for $1795 at its introduction, now sells for $1595 with the coming introduction of the KayPro 4 and KayPro 10.

Exciting, recently introduced machines may be immune from discounts. The IBM Personal Computer was one of these when it first appeared, but it isn't now. The Epson QX-10 is only sold for full list, even by mail order, because demand currently outstrips production.

Your chances of getting a discount are enhanced if you discuss with the sales rep a system price, including all the peripherals and software you will need in the immediate future. You can use the sales rep's unwillingness to offer a discount on the computer itself as leverage to lower the price of a printer, or to include free software packages, disks, and paper.

Do not be afraid to walk away from the sales rep if the price of the system cannot be reduced to the amount you can afford. Do not be afraid that you are taking bread from the mouths of the sales rep's children. Chances are the sales rep is already taking their welfare into account.

Do come prepared to buy the system immediately, or within a week. If you've gotten a good deal, you must take advantage of it before it evaporates. If you're not ready to buy, say that you're just looking. The salespeople don't want to be put through a hard bargaining session only to find out you want to buy sometime six months from now. Six months from now, the price you've just negotiated will no longer be good, and the sales reps, quite rightly, won't take you seriously.

Any quote you receive should be good for at least a week or ten days, up to a month if you cement the deal with a deposit of several hundred dollars. This gives the sales representative time to assemble and test your system components, and gives you time to pull the money together.

To Sum Up

The kind of VSB you start will depend at least in part on your financial situation. The kind of computer system you want depends at least in part on the kind of VSB you are planning to operate. Make sure your planned VSB is compatible with your present financial situation.

Mail-order buying is risky for hardware and peripherals, but okay if you're careful and if you know what you want. For software and supplies, mail order is probably the best way to buy.

Buying a computer system takes money, but probably not as much money as you fear. For one thing, Uncle Sam is willing to subsidize part of your investment.

You don't have to buy new equipment. You don't have to pay list prices. And you don't have to break your piggy bank to get the cash.

You can borrow the money from a bank or from your credit card or life insurance policy. You can lease the equipment from the bank; this comes down to borrowing the money in the long run.

Or you can simply borrow the computer from your

friendly college or university, until you are in a position to buy your own.

Whatever method you choose to acquire a computer, or the use of one, a properly planned and properly run VSB will buy it for you. This may seem unbelievable, but it is true.

We know. We've done it. To find out how—

TURN THE PAGE.

CHAPTER 3

It's Not What You CAN Do, It's What You WANT to Do

Success . . . and *sigh* failure

We know. You're still nervous about starting your VSB. You're probably thinking, "This hardware stuff is fine, but what do I *do* with it? How do I *choose* what to do? What if I fail? I could, you know, no matter what you folks say."

You're right, of course, so let's slow down a bit and start thinking about what you're going to do.

The answer is this: Whatever you want to do.

Honest.

There are plenty of business opportunities out there, right under your nose, and in the next chapter we're going to show you how to find the ones that are right for you—but first you must decide to succeed. And you must decide what to succeed *at.* We'll help, but we can't decide for you. Your success is your own responsibility.

Pretty frightening, no?

Success, in fact, is the only thing more frightening than failure. It forces you to decide what to do next. The problem with *deciding* to succeed, to risk something for eventual gain, is this: What if you fail?

That fear comes from a place deep in all our psyches; our species has been carrying it around for millennia.

It all goes back tens of thousands of years, to when our primate ancestors were running around trying to find food and get away from predators. Back then, "success" meant "having enough food so that I won't starve right now" or "getting up a tree before that sabertooth eats me."

"Failure" meant dying.

The imprinting went deep. Even today, people still drive themselves to mental and physical illness over fear of failure. The "businessman's ulcer" is only one example.

But it can be different now. And it should be. Your VSB doesn't have to stand between you and immediate starvation. Whether or not you're successful in your VSB, nobody's going to eat you. Your VSB *can* make your life better. It might eventually free you from the necessity of holding down a regular job. But it isn't a matter of life and death.

So relax. If at first you don't succeed at your VSB, the world will continue to turn. You'll continue to live and prosper. Your money machine and your VSB can be very important to you, but only important-good-or-not-so-good, not important-good-or-very-bad.

That ancestral primate imprinting doesn't apply here.

Finding the Happy People

What *does* apply here is happiness, and what kinds of people are happy. Think about it for a moment. What single group of people is, by and large, the happiest?

The richest, you say? No, that's not true. Rich people can be just as unhappy as anybody else.

Probably the happiest people you know make their living, or a part of it, in relatively offbeat jobs. They have the sorts of jobs that other people haven't pushed them into, jobs that don't pay terribly well or have a lot of status. No mother raises a son or daughter to be a macrame weaver, a fiddle player, a poet, or a free-lance writer.

There's a reason: The people who do those jobs do them simply because they like them; they enjoy what they do for its own sake, not for the sake of the rewards those jobs may bring.

Of course, there are a lot of people with high-paying and high-status jobs who *are* happy. But when they are, it's not because of the status and the dollars; those are nice extras. Happy doctors and lawyers and investment counselors enjoy practicing medicine or law or finance.

Happy people enjoy what they're doing—for its own sake.

Whether they are multimillionaire Wall Street brokers or impoverished candlemakers, they are doing what they want to do.

You can, too. Certainly, somewhere among the things you can do well and enjoy there is some task that your computer may be able to help you do.

All you have to do is what you want to do.

But before that can happen, you've got to decide what you want to do.

Answer this question quickly: What do you want to do?

Did you hem and haw a bit? That isn't unusual. Figuring out what you want to do isn't all that simple.

But there is a way to figure it out. . . .

How to Figure Out What You Want to Do

First: List What You've Done

We're not talking about what VSB you're going to establish. For now, let's just figure out what you like to do. Not what services you're going to provide—term paper typing, doing newsletters, balancing neighbors' checkbooks for pay—but which skills you enjoy using.

Some of those may surprise you.

You're going to start by making some lists. Use your database management system if you'd like, or your word-processing program, or even a pencil and paper. But if you use the latter, get a lot of sheets. These are going to be long lists.

You'll need a bit of quiet and privacy for this. Get it. Turn off the phone, put the cat out, ask your mate to take in a movie . . . whatever. Pour yourself a tall, cool drink, or a cup of coffee if you'd prefer, and relax with this book for a while.

Got your system running, or your pencil in hand? Are you sitting in a comfortable chair?

Great. Now let's start making lists.

The first thing you'll list is: everything you've ever done.

Yes, *everything*. Not just the full-time and part-time jobs you've held, or the volunteer work you've gotten involved in, or your hobbies—although you'll include all of those—but *everything*.

Forget about money, forget about computers, forget about VSBs, about success and failure, about what you want to do or are afraid of doing, or what your neighbors wouldn't want you doing on the front lawn because it might scare the horses.

Forget it. Nobody's going to see this list except you. Plan to get rid of it when you're done, if that will help you keep yourself honest.

Don't be afraid to be silly here, or any time that you're brainstorming. Silliness is harmless. It's not going to matter if there are dumb things on the list. What matters is how many good, applicable skills there are on it.

We'll worry about that later, but for now, just list; let things roll out of your subconscious. If you hear a voice in the back of your head saying, "This won't do any good," or "That's immoral, illegal, and liable to get me shot if I do it again," or "I can't do that well," **ignore it.** List.

Part of your list might end up looking something like this:

Things I've Done

Bank teller
Secretary
Shopping for food
Volleyball
Checkers
Buying a computer
Playing Go Fish
Swearing at a computer
Fishing
Cleaning fish
Cooking
Cleaning a house
Making stinkbombs
Watching rockets
Taking photographs
Breathing
Admiring sunsets
Planting flowers
Swimming
Sawing wood
Cleaning soot from the chimney
Burning wood
Hitting my brother with a hammer
Petting a cat
Playing cards
Student
Playing house
Writing letters
Housekeeper
Reading books
Building a bookcase
Sex
Grocery clerk
Being a parent
Watching TV
Being a child
Lifeguard

That's not a complete list, of course. Everybody has done many, many more things than that.

If your list isn't at least five times as long as this one, either you've led a very limited life or you're cheating. Go back and do it again, until you're sure you've listed everything you've ever done in your life.

If you didn't include "talking to people" and "listening to people," go back and do it yet again.

Second: Discover Your Skills

Hidden in that list of things you've done are the skills you have. If the list is complete, you've included all of them. Now it's time to pry them out.

Yes, and list them.

Take your time with this; some of them won't come easily. As you go over your list, think back. Try to figure out what skills you had to use when you did things.

Let's take an example that applies to everyone—being a student. We've all been students at one time or another. Some of us never stop.

Being a student requires a whole galaxy of skills:

Keeping to a schedule
Following directions
Reading
Understanding
Writing
Typing
Working with others
Creative lying ("The dog ate my paper")
Doing mathematical calculations
Explaining your failures to others ("Well, Dad, it seems the gym teacher was flunking everyone with curly hair")
Doing line drawings
Sweeping up glass after you've shattered a beaker in chem lab
Fudging results
Research
Obeying rules
Breaking rules
Talking your way out of it when you've been caught breaking rules
Buttering teachers up
Using a rubber band to spang paper clip halves off the venetian blinds

That's only a partial list. It could go on for pages.

Make a "skills list" for everything you've done. While the other list was long, this one should be immense.

Now, let's boil the list down a bit.

Third: Decide Which Skills You Like to Use

Go through that list of skills, and circle the things that you really enjoyed doing—not for the rewards, but for the sake of doing them. Don't ask yourself if these are skills you're good at using, but only whether or not you like using them.

You may surprise yourself here. You may find that you really did enjoy the time you used a lathe to turn out a single chair leg, even though you never finished making the chair.

You may have gotten a lot of pleasure out of typing class, or painting the walls, or adding a column of numbers together and having it come out right, or almost anything.

Whatever it is that you enjoy, list it, and think about it. Then take the next step:

Fourth: Decide What You Do Well

Take all those skills you've enjoyed using and sort them into two categories: (1) those you do well (not perfectly, just well), and (2) those you don't do well.

Self-honesty, while important to the whole process, is critical here. This isn't some sort of Ten Commandments pitch; we're not saying that you shouldn't ever tell a fib. But right here and now, you have to be straight with yourself.

Because being dishonest with yourself is just begging for trouble. As an example, let's look at a skill that has obvious commercial possibilities: typing.

Later on, you might find yourself being offered a term paper typing job—a ten-thousand-word paper, say, for a dollar and a half per page.

At 25Ø words per double-spaced page, that comes out to forty pages. You'd get sixty dollars.

If your typing speed really is fifty words per minute, and if you can actually keep that up for an hour at a stretch, this one job would take you a little more than three one-hour sessions. Since you should always be a bit conservative, let's say that it would take you four one-hour sessions to earn that sixty dollars.

That's fifteen dollars an hour, which is not too bad.

But what if your real speed is only half what you think it is? Then, your income would only be seven-fifty an hour—not quite so good.

And what if you really can't keep up that speed for longer than fifteen minutes at a time? What if you need at least a ten-minute break between typing sessions? Your earnings go down again.

And what if you're still trying to hold down your full-time job, but you've agreed to do six of these term papers by the end of the week?

Three possibilities: either you're not going to keep your commitments, or you're going to drive yourself into physical exhaustion . . . or both.

No fun. Your customers will be upset. You're not going

to do a very clean job under that kind of pressure. You'll be tired *and* upset. Your boss at your regular job won't be thrilled, either.

All because you lied to yourself about something as trivial as your typing speed.

Now, in this example, if you had been honest with yourself, you might have decided to charge more per page—if you could get it—or to take on less work, or that the money your time and effort were earning wasn't worth the trouble.

By lying to yourself, you're just endangering yourself.

So be honest, and be objective here. Think back, as you go over the skills you enjoy. Ask yourself some hard questions: Am I really good at this? Have other people thought I was good at this? Do I remember getting good grades or promotions or raises or compliments when I used this skill? Do other people who use this skill value my advice?

With a bit of honesty, you'll sort this list of skills you like using into two categories: the skills you enjoy using and are good at, and the skills you enjoy using but aren't good at.

For both categories, there's a common next step:

Fifth: Polish Your Skills

Your computer may be able to help you here. CAI (Computer Assisted Instruction) programs are available for many business-related skills. CAI is a growing industry; more courses are becoming available all the time, so keep your eyes open. Get the catalogue from any software house, and look over the Instructional Programs section closely. See if there's a course that ties in with skills you have—or wish you had—and want to polish.

There may be some skills you enjoy, but that you're sure can't establish any connection between *you* and *money*.

You may be right. You may be wrong. It's not time to worry about making money yet, anyway. Polish the skills. It never hurts to be good at something. And it's always good to be the best at *anything*. There is nothing so trivial as putting a little white ball into a small hole in the grass, but Arnold Palmer doesn't seem to be starving.

Often, you can find mentors, people who are good at something you want to be better at, and who—for money, for thanks, for the fun of teaching a skill they've mastered—can and will teach you.

Don't neglect the power of play. Your computer is a great toy and a great teacher at the same time. Play around with it. Fiddle with different sorts of programs. You might learn—or get fascinated and frustrated enough to force yourself to learn—enough about programming to give yourself the germ of a new and profitable idea.

Let yourself get a bit irritated with a bug in your word-processing program, and try to find out why it doesn't do what it should. Program patches are worth some money; knowledge is worth a lot more.

Fool around with different kinds of outputs. You might find something that would give a computer-generated newsletter a unique and interesting look.

Odds are, some skill or other is going to catch your fancy, and it'll be difficult to hold yourself back from finding out everything you can about it. You'll *want* to polish that skill until it shines. Whether or not you were good at it, you'll be *great* at it.

Then take the next step:

Sixth: Gather Your Nerve

We're back where we started: fear of failure and fear of success.

Look, if you absolutely refuse to take a risk, there's nothing this book can do for you. There's nothing anyone can do for you. Success requires a willingness to take a few risks.

And as we started this chapter by telling you, we're not talking here about risking your life, or even your fortune. We're talking about using your computer to set up a Very Small Business with a small initial investment. If you already have your computer, you probably won't need to invest more than a couple of hundred dollars.

We're not asking you to risk a whole lot. There's no need to be nervous on that account.

But you still may have legitimate reasons to be a bit apprehensive. You may be asking yourself, "Who said I could do this and be successful?"

Good question. Our society is set up to give people licenses to do some things. Implicitly, it denies permission to everyone else. All kinds of secular priesthoods have been set up.

In some cases, this makes sense. You don't want someone opening up your skull if he or she isn't a certified brain surgeon with umpty-ump years of training, and a diploma that says he or she is capable of doing that, and doing it well. You wouldn't want someone to defend you in court if that someone hadn't demonstrated a lot of knowledge about the law and the judicial system.

If you want to be a brain surgeon or a defense attorney, you're going to have to go out and get not only the skills but the permissions those professions demand.

You need permissions in big business, too. You won't have a shot at the presidency of ITT if you don't have an MBS degree. You'll never get into top management.

That's in *big* business. But in small business—and most particularly in Very Small Business—the two things that most determine whether or not you can succeed are what you know, and how hard and *intelligently* you are willing to work. You don't need permission. You need skills and determination.

A bit of whimsical curiosity wouldn't hurt, either.

Seventh: Turn On the Money Machine

How? To start,

TURN THE PAGE.

CHAPTER 4

Turning On the Money Machine

How to Set Up Your Own Small Business

By now you have acquired the computer equipment you will need (or have mapped out a strategy for obtaining it, *gratis* or otherwise), and are thoroughly familiar with what it can do. You have also decided which of your skills you're going to call upon to make that lovely little machine of yours pay for itself. Most importantly, you've got your courage cranked up and are ready to take the gamble of starting your own Very Small Business.

Okay, let's do it!

The first step is to identify your product. It sounds obvious, of course, since you've already picked the skill you're going to use, but your *skill* and your *product* are two different things.

Put your machine in word-processing mode, and type out your special talent. Now list all the goods and/or services you can possibly produce with it. Go a little crazy here. Release the power of your subconscious; don't hamper it with self-imposed censorship. The technique is called brainstorming, and it succeeds only if you don't criticize your ideas while you're generating them. There's time enough later to discard the nonsense. This is the moment to be creative, even silly. (If you can't awaken that creativity lying dormant in your soul, Chapter 6 does go into a few possibilities in some detail.)

After half an hour or so, your screen ought to look like Figure 1.

```
      B:MM4   PAGE 3 LINE 1 COL 01                INSERT ON   LINE SPACING 2
L----!----!----!----!----!----!----!----!----!----!----!----!--------R
                                                                          <
                           ^BMy skill is TYPING^B                         <
                                                                          <
                                                                          <
With it I can:                                                            <
                                                                          <
     Type letters for illiterates.                                        <
     Do my neighbors' Christmas card lists.                               <
     Type term papers and theses for college students.                    <
     Send the same letter to my grandmother once a month for the rest of her
life.                                                                     <
     Prepare long boiler-plate documents that need to have variable information
inserted in them at various predetermined points.                         <
     Do mass mailings for local businesses/political parties/charities.   <
     Become a local business/political party/charity.                     <
     Send my grandmother's letter to everyone I know once a month for the rest
of their lives.                                                           <
     "Set type" (i.e., prepare camera-ready copy with justified columns) for
local newsletters that either use a regular typewriter or have printers do it
for them.                                                                 <
     Start a newsletter of my own and find people to write for it.        <
```

Figure 1.

Once you've made your list, go over it, think about the possibilities, and then choose the one that you think you're most likely to enjoy.

That's right, just one. Time enough later for diversifying—there's all the rest of your life for that.

At this point, stop. Consult a lawyer (expensive) or your state attorney general's office (usually free, but much more frustrating) to find out if any laws regulate the sale of your product. Each state has different laws. It is beyond the scope of this book to list all the ways in which each of the states regulates the sale of goods and services.

All legal? Great. Now identify your market. Who will pay you cold hard cash for your product?

Let's assume that from the list in Figure 1 you've selected "Prepare long boiler-plate documents that need to have variable information inserted in them at various predetermined points."

Sit down with your Yellow Pages. Start at the beginning and examine each heading. Leaf through the entire book. Every time you come to a new category, ask yourself if, based on what you know, this type of business is likely to need your service.

If you haven't the foggiest idea, but the occupation sounds interesting, give one of the companies a call and ask whoever answers the phone if they do boiler-plate documents. Most people like to talk about their jobs (even if only to complain). As long as you're polite, friendly, and sound interested, the odds are you'll get your answer pretty quickly.

So you're flipping through the Yellow Pages and you come to ATTORNEYS. Hmm. They do contracts, wills, divorces, evictions, repossessions . . . the list of actions they undertake that require the insertion of variable information into boiler-plate documents seems almost endless.

You decide you're going to aim at lawyers, first. Next month or next year you can branch out. This is a starting point, and nothing more.

So, keeping your market firmly in mind, you identify yourself. That's right. Give your VSB a name. It's time for the Yellow Pages again. Look under COMPUTERS, COMPUTER SERVICES, and so on—this time to find the names you should not use. Avoid anything that sounds even vaguely similar to another company's. Whenever you come up with one you like, cross-reference into the White Pages. It's easier to pass over a nifty name than to defend a legal suit for using someone else's. (See also the list of software companies in Part IV of this book.)

Toy with names that sound as though they might appeal to your specialized market. Restaurants are not likely to use a bookkeeping service called Cooked Books, no matter how cute it sounds to you. Doctors will probably avoid anything with a "quack" in it. But lawyers might go for Lawyers' Aid. Who knows?

If all else fails, consider your own name or initials in combination with the product—Smith's Word Processing or KKT MailLists, or something along those lines.

Try the name out on a few close friends. If any wince, or laugh aloud, you might want to consider a new one. . . .

Are any of your friends strong in the graphic arts? Maybe one will help you design a logo. If not, we recommend that you forget about a logo for the time being, and just go with your VSB's name.

Once you've settled on a skill, a product, a market, and a name, it's time to get going—but for God's sake, don't mortgage the house to raise the capital to rent an office and equip it with sleek Scandinavian furniture. Unless you've picked the kind of business where the customer must come to you (and frankly, at this stage of the game, you shouldn't have), you don't need a fancy office.

What you do need is a place where you can work. For peace of mind, it should either be far removed from the rest of your household, or have good solid doors. Privacy is essential. You'll soon feel paranoid if you can't leave materials lying around because someone will be eating breakfast on your desk.

Good utilities are a must. You'll want a dedicated power line for your computer and its peripherals (unless you *like* dealing with diskette errors caused by the dishwasher's kicking in), plenty of light, heat in the winter and air conditioning in the summer, decent ventilation, and a telephone jack. Right now, by the way, you do *not* need a second telephone number. Later on, perhaps, but for now a ten-dollar extension phone will do.

For tax purposes, you should use your office for absolutely nothing but your VSB. If you work at your kitchen table, the IRS will disallow all deductions you take for an office in the home. If you convert the spare bedroom and don't have too many overnight guests, you're on firmer footing. If you clear out a corner of your basement, throw a desk in, and remember not to store the storm windows there during the summer, you're safe. For a more detailed discussion of this and other tax-related matters, see Part III, Chapter 11.

You will need ledgers—either the time-honored bound ledgers available in any good stationery store, or electronic ledgers you create yourself with one of the spreadsheets available.

A very simple spreadsheet ledger would look something like Figure 2 (page 53).

Next you need time—a certain number of hours per day or per week or per month (you make the choice; remember, you're your own boss now) which you promise yourself you will devote to your work.

Finally, you need the tools of your trade—and what they will be depends entirely on what your product is. A mailing list service, for example, might require a cheap, fast printer (some sort of dot-matrix) with a pin-feed platen; many, many, many varieties of labels; blank diskettes for storing your customers' files; the software package to input, sort, and output the lists; invoice forms . . . whatever.

It's time now to make your first visit to a printer. You should have business cards and letterhead stationery and envelopes. Eventually you will need much more—eventually you will make so many visits to the printer's that he'll begin to feel like family—but we're starting small here, and bootstrapping our way up. Bills can go out on letterhead stationery. Honest. Nobody minds.

By the way; should you be just a tad strapped for cash, consider making your own letterhead stationery. You've got the computer, yes? And the word-processing package that will give you nifty boldfaces and doublestrikes and variable character widths and all that, yes?

Use it. Flick on your machine and spend an hour or two playing with its features. Try typing your name, let us say, using eight-pitch boldfaced and doublestruck capital let-

	A	B	C	D	E	F
1	DATE	Check #	Payer/Payee	Income	Outgo	Balance
2	------	------	------	------	------	------
3			Carryover May			969.83
4	840601	1003	Gas Co (1/6)		8.47	961.37
5	840601	1004	Electric (1/6)		13.98	947.39
6	840601	1005	Water (1/6)		2.81	944.57
7	840602	1006	Rent (1/6)		50.00	894.57
8	840603	5368	Carey's Caterers	75.00		969.57
9	840604	245	Atty LeGree/evict	100.00		1069.57
10	840605	1007	Midnight Off. Supp		76.88	992.69
11			(box 8" discs)			992.69
12	840607	cash	mileage to			992.69
13			Hal's Eats =			992.69
14			19 miles*2*.20		7.60	985.09
15	840607	733	Hal's Eats	200.00		1185.09
16	840608	1008	RS232C cable		28.18	1156.91
17	840609	48	Term paper--RLT	75.00		1231.91
18	840611	1009	Bell		23.00	1208.91
19	840612	1010	MCI		27.98	1180.93
20	840613	1011	Yoknapatawpha Times		10.00	1170.93
21	840614	1012	IBM:1 case ribbons		107.50	1063.43
22	840615	3979	Nag-o-gram			1063.43
23			--Isaiah O'Neill	10.00		1073.43
24	840616	53	Rewrite RLT	7.50		1080.93
25	840617	1013	Car insurnce (1/10)		5.00	1075.93
26	840618	1014	Business lunch		9.23	1066.70
27			@ McDonald's			1066.70
28	840619	1015	100 stamps/USPS		20.00	1046.70
29	840620	3983	Rpt nag-o-gram	5.00		1051.70
30			--I O'N			1051.70
31	840621	8593	Ph.D.Thss Deposit	100.00		1151.70
32			--FH			1151.70
33	840622	37	Poetry chapbok	250.00		1401.70
34			--eec			1401.70
35	840623	37952603	Rep Party nwsltr	500.00		1901.70
36	840624	12	Dem's nwsltr (!!)	50.00		1951.70
37	840625	35683	House of Pain	47.50		1999.20
38			-- ad copy			1999.20
39	------	------	------	------	------	------
40	Totals			1420.00	390.63	1999.20

Figure 2.

ters, centered at the top of your sheet of paper. Do the same with your address and phone number at the bottom of the page. Boldfaced equal signs made to overlap give you peachy parallel lines.

You can do the same with your envelopes, too. And save a little bit of money at a time when you probably haven't got a whole lot to throw around.

Figure 3 gives a few examples of what an hour with a Xerox 820-II, a Diablo 630 printer, and four different print-wheels can do for you.

But let's assume here that your pockets are stuffed

very small business

123 Main Street Anytown, ST 68000 (111) 555-1212

CRAIG'S COMPUTERIZED CPA SERVICES
4567 ELM STREET YOURCITY, ST 98765
(222) 555-1212

```
*****************************************************************
\ | /                                          FBN Star Trackers
--< >--                                   Electronic Horoscopes
/ | \                                       Post Office Box 555
                                         Fadeout City, ST 12345
*****************************************************************
```

T. Jane Doe
Computer Consultant
(333) 555-1212

9201 First Avenue
Hometown, ST 43210

Santa's Little Helper
3456 Third Street
Ourhamlet, ST 67890
(444) 555-1212

Figure 3.

with greenery and you have no desire to create your own stationery.

Off you go to the nearest printshop, right?

Wrong.

Down you sit, Yellow Pages open to the section marked PRINTERS, telephone by your hand, computer turned on with your database management system (DBMS) up and running.

See, the thing about printers is, for any given job, the cheapest will charge about a third of what the most expensive one does, while the highest-priced guy will not necessarily do the best job for you.

So, depending on what DBMS you have, you set up a quick and dirty database with eleven fields: Firm Name, Phone Number, Worth Doing Business With, Quote-Giver's Name, Business Card Minimum Quantity, Stationery Minimum Quantity, Envelope Minimum Quantity, Card Price, Stationery Price, Envelope Price, and Total Price. (Have the system compute it for you.)

Even though the per-unit price plummets when you order larger quantities, we're dealing in minimums here because, let's face it, you are going to change your mind about how good your material looks after you've used it for a while. If your business catches fire (in either sense of the phrase), your address will change. You'll grow dissatisfied with your logo. Maybe you'll even rename your VSB.

We guarantee you this: you do not want to purchase ten thousand business cards right now, no matter what kind of deal the printer will make you on them. It's much easier to toss fifty unused cards in the garbage than ninety-eight hundred.

You call the first name—AAAAA Printshop Inc., let us say—and while the phone is ringing you type the name and phone number into your DBMS. You tell the person who answers, "I need some business cards, some letterhead stationery, and some envelopes. Can I get a quote?"

If the person says "No," say "Thank you," hang up, and put an *N* in the Worth Doing Business With field.

If the person says "You'll have to come in for that," say "I see," hang up, and put an *N* in the Worth Doing Business With field.

The person who says "Sure, what do you want?" is the one you want to talk to. Put a *Y* in that firm's Worth Doing Business With field. Ask about the minimum quantity of each item you can purchase, and enter that information into your DBMS. Tell the printer exactly what you want, specifying sizes (8½″ by 11″ is standard paper size), paper weights, color, whether you want it embossed or engraved or offset. . . . Then type into your DBMS the prices for each.

We strongly recommend that you dial your way through the entire book. You will be surprised at the incredible discrepancies in prices and quantities. You will have to bite your tongue to keep from laughing when someone quotes you a price of fifty dollars for five hundred sheets of letterhead stationery, envelopes extra.

All done?

If you would rather deal with only one printer, have your DBMS sort on the Total Cost field, and go in person to talk to the five printers who offered the lowest prices for the entire package.

If you don't mind dealing with several printers, have your DBMS sort three times, once for each cost field, and each time print out the five lowest companies.

When you go, ask to see samples of their work. A print shop without hundreds of stunning samples lying around is either in its first week of business, or to be shunned. Ask how long the job will take. Ask what happens if the job is not done to your liking.

This will all take time, but you'll meet a lot of interesting people. And in the end, you'll have, we trust, filled your basic stationery requirements, and acquired a much better knowledge of what's available to you in the printing field.

Oh, yeah, one other thing: when you're done, you'll have a snazzy little database of printers ready for adaptation and future use.

How to Find Work and Start to Make Money: Advertising and Marketing Techniques

Before you can start to advertise, you must determine whether to use a rifle or a shotgun. Your market is clearly a distinct subset of the general population—if only because you think it needs your product—but are there other ways to single out the individuals who comprise it? Doctors, for example, are lumped together in the Yellow Pages. *Pac-Man* players are not. A city directory lists everyone who lives on a certain street, but not everyone who wants recipe files maintained. Schools often publish directories of students and faculty members, but not of people who want to learn programming and aren't enrolled anywhere.

If the individuals who might buy your product are clearly identifiable, you'll probably want to use the telephone and the mails as your primary means of advertising.

If, however, your potential customers are submerged in the general population, you should start thinking about newspapers, magazines, and other means of mass advertising.

Telephone Solicitation

If you have a reasonably good voice, think well on your feet, and have a fair amount of self-confidence (but then, if you didn't have that last, you probably wouldn't be going into business for yourself, would you?), consider the telephone. Properly used, it is an extremely valuable sales tool.

In many areas, a phone call is cheaper than a first-class stamp. It's quicker than an in-person visit (and you needn't dress up for it, either). It's harder to overlook than a newspaper ad. And frequently, Ma Bell has already given you, absolutely free, one neat little list of all your market's telephone numbers.

But be realistic. You are not going to close deals with strangers over the phone. A call might suffice to get business from someone who already knows you, but with anyone else, your goal is to make an appointment to sit down and talk things over face to face.

So haul out the Yellow Pages again, switch on your computer, and run your DBMS. At an absolute minimum, you're going to want to enter into your own database the name, mailing address, and phone number of everyone you have spoken to. More fields would be nice: Date of First Phone Call, for example, Date on Which to Call Back, Degree of Interest Expressed—any kind of further information that would help you deal with this potential client. Now dial the number.

It rings.

The secretary answers.

Do you deliver your pitch?

The first rule of telephone solicitation is to speak to the person who makes the decisions. Most secretaries—not all, but most—do not make the decisions.

In our example of boiler-plate documents for lawyers, you clearly want to talk with the attorneys themselves.

To avoid having to fight your way through the screens thrown up by protective secretaries/receptionists, time your calls: make them early in the morning, before the secretaries have come to work; during the lunch hours; or shortly after the close of the business day. This heightens the odds that the decision-maker will answer the phone.

If you do run into someone who wants to know why you're calling before putting you through, it often helps to ask a question that must be answered by facts or plans the secretary does not have. Something on the order of, "Well, I'd like to determine Attorney Brown's business objectives, and his strategies for obtaining a larger market share." If you're polite and friendly, you will be connected with the boss.

Once you have the decision-maker on the phone, you have ten seconds to make a good impression. Clearly, you need a snazzy opening line: ten seconds' worth of patter that will convince your listener that you're worth further attention. In our running example, you could try something to the effect of "Good morning, counselor. My name is Joe Smith, and I'd like to show you a way to save time and money with absolutely no initial investment."

Some telephone solicitors write out everything they are going to say and read it over the phone. We do not recommend this as a regular practice. It leads to a singsong delivery that robs your words of meaning and creates a bad initial impression—exactly the opposite of what you want to accomplish. You might need to read from a script for your first five or ten calls—until you get comfortable with the notion of phoning complete strangers and subjecting them to a sales pitch—but after that you should throw away the script and *talk* to the person at the other end of the line.

Do, however, type out a brief key-word or topical outline of your pitch. Sooner or later you will endure that embarrassing moment when your mind goes blank and you can't remember for the life of you whom you're talking to or how far along you have gotten. Jot down phrases and ideas that you find yourself succeeding with, too.

A list of objections to your product is especially useful. Start it before you begin phoning. Type up the objections you expect to hear, and work out a short, coherent, compelling riposte for each of them. Every time you hear a new one, take a break from the phoning to figure out how best to answer it. Keep the objections and responses on file. Eventually you'll know them all by heart—but until you do, you could lose out on a lot of potential business.

Be positive in your approach. *Assume* that the person is going to want to talk to you. Don't say, "May I sit down and explain this to you?" Instead, say, "Would Monday be a good day for us to get together, or would Tuesday be better?"

Be creative when you're dealing with potential customers. If that hypothetical attorney says he already has a word processor, so he doesn't need you, ask him if he ever needs help when his secretaries are sick or on vacation, for example, or during peak work periods.

A lot of people will try to put you off by asking you to send informative brochures. How precisely to deal with the request is a matter of personal style, but keep in mind that acceding to it is probably a waste of time. One sales rep of our acquaintance replies to that question brashly: "Hey look, we both know that if I send you a brochure, you'll toss it out without reading it. Let's sit down together. If, after five minutes, you decide I'm wasting your time, toss me out. But I assure you that the time will be well spent." She says the line works. It reassures potential customers that they haven't committed to anything yet, and it lets her get her foot in the door.

A nice touch—and an easy one, since you've pumped name, address, and so forth into your DBMS at the beginning of the call—is immediately to print out a sales letter when you hang up. Don't, for God's sake, fill a page with one single-spaced paragraph; a brief note will do. The idea is to lodge further your name and product in the other person's mind, and to give that person at least a vague impression of quality and competence.

If you've set an appointment, mention the time and date as a gentle reminder, and use some subtle hype to get the customer excited about seeing you.

Should you have failed, express your gratitude, boost your product a little, and urge whoever it is to get in touch with you. Don't be so pushy that you turn the account off, but don't roll over and play dead, either. People do change their minds.

Even when people won't see you, ask if they know anyone else who might be interested in your service. If you pose the question properly, you can get your leads to generate other leads for you. Don't hang up empty-handed. Try to get something from every call you make.

When your pitch *doesn't* work, examine it. Try to figure out why. Poor delivery? Bad logic? Lack of pizzazz? Wrong target for that product? Wrong market for that product? Now, remember to be realistic: you're not going to set an appointment with each call, and you shouldn't succumb to despair just because someone wouldn't see you. If, however, person after person after person evinces absolutely no interest in what you're selling, it's probably time to go back to Square One and start all over.

By the way, after making all these calls, you're going to find yourself with a nifty-keen database all ready for mass mailings. Speaking of which . . .

Mass Mailings

Whom to Send To

Direct mail is absolutely and without question worthwhile *if* you can identify your potential market. Clearly, if you're aiming at doctors or lawyers or candlestick makers, good ol' Ma Bell has already done the work for you. Crank up your DBMS, pump the names and addresses into it, and you're all set.

Other sources have names of people who might be interested in your product. If you're looking to provide a product or service to people in your area who themselves own or rent computers, talk to your local computer stores. Naturally, anybody trying to make a buck off the same product you've picked for your VSB is not too likely to be helpful, but if you're offering something they don't offer, something that makes a computer a more attractive purchase for the average person, you might find a surprising amount of cooperation.

Besides, it never hurts to ask.

Clubs and associations often release the names of their members—sometimes for free, sometimes for a small charge. Again, ask. All they can say is no.

And don't forget to check your Yellow Pages for major mail-list firms. There's usually a minimum order, but rarely is it so high as to break the bank. Many of them have WATS numbers; most of them have customer service representatives who are paid to help you find the mailing list you want. Call them. Tell them what kind of person you're looking for. They might well be able to break out a list of people with zip codes in your area who have purchased tricycles by mail in the last eighteen months. And if that's where you think your market is—go for it!

While we're on the subject, one very important reminder: get the name and mailing address of everyone you deal with, so you can put them on a mailing list you generate yourself.

What to Send Them

First you have to decide your goal: Are you trying to get them to buy through the mail, or are you trying to get them to call you and set up an appointment? Generally, if you're selling "goods" as opposed to a service, you want them to reply with a check. If you're selling a service, you either want them to phone you, or you're paving the way for a call of your own.

The Mail Sale

If you're selling goods—new software, custom hardware, supplies, or the like—send your potential customers the best possible description of your product that you can afford to assemble. You want to mail them a collage of words and pictures that will drive them immediately to fill out the order form you've enclosed and return it in the envelope you've also enclosed.

As you're putting the package together, be aware that unless you come across as unique, your mailing will not succeed. People are inundated with junk mail today. A catalogue that looks just like every other catalogue is *not* going to pay for itself.

So stress your differences. Emphasize whatever it is that makes you unique and *better*. Remember, the people getting this don't know you from Adam. If they're reasonably rational, they're going to be a little leery of sending you money.

When you've compiled the package, roll out your DBMS with the file of printers, and start talking to them. Shop around once again.

A few suggestions: Do *not* use a post office box. A brand-new VSB with a return address of PO Box ### might as well call itself Fly By Night Incorporated. Use your home address. So maybe you get some people stopping in to check you out—so what? Sell them something while they're there.

Use plain English. Forget that you went to Harvard and haven't used a word of less than four syllables since you graduated. Save that for alumni reunions. When the average person requires a dictionary to understand what his junk mail is saying, he does not buy.

Do, absolutely positively definitely, include as your order form something they can cut out, fill in with their name and address, and return to you. God only knows why, but people like to cut things out and write their names and addresses on them. You'll find your response rate increases significantly when you include one, and drops when you don't.

On that cutout you should include, again in plain English, a quasi-contract between you and the buyer. We used to publish a magazine for science fiction writers, and all our cutouts included phrasing to this effect: "All right, I need *Empire*, so sign me up right now! Enclosed is my check/money order in the sum $______ for the subscription and back issues I have checked."

And it worked.

Of course, we had a unique product.

And a mailer that described it beautifully.

Which we sent to carefully selected lists of people.

But that's what it's all about.

Selling Services?

This is more difficult. What you're aiming at here is *not* a large check by return mail, but simply to tell people that you exist. And maybe to provoke a few inquiring phone calls, during which you can set an appointment to go in and talk to them. That's when you're really going to sell them your service.

In this case we recommend that you skip the fancy package. Load whatever merge-print program comes with your word-processing software, and send an individualized form letter to everyone in your database of potential customers.

Keep the letter short and simple. All you want these folks to do is call and ask to see you. So: introduce yourself and your product briefly, plant some sort of hook to pique their interest, and repeat your phone number.

Very few will call back. Sad, but true. But don't be discouraged.

Let a week go by, and call *them*. First review the section on telephone solicitation, and go to it.

Do not write off those who don't bite. *Today* they're not buying. Next month they might be.

Cross off your list only those people who already have computers, and who already provide for themselves the service you're trying to sell.

Every month or two run off a batch of letters—making certain that each generation of letter is markedly different from all of its predecessors—and mail them out.

Persistence is what does it.

Still Don't Know Your Market's Identity?

If your potential customers are so thoroughly hidden in the general population that neither Ma Bell nor the mailing-list companies can identify them, it's time to try newspaper and/or magazine advertising. If finances are tight, start with a classified ad.

The odds are you're aiming at people in your immediate area, so talk to the advertising people at all the local newspapers. Ask them whom they reach. (Believe us, they know.)

If you've got the budget, go for display ads—and remember to include a coupon someone can cut out and return to you. Number One, people like to do that, and Number Two, when they do it, you get their names.

Many areas have regional magazines. Talk to their advertising managers, as well.

If you can't put names to your market, and you haven't got the bucks for newspaper/magazine advertising, but you do know where your market shops, try printing up a poster and leaving it where it will be visible. Computer stores if you're trying to reach computer owners, supermarkets for the average person, school corridors . . . use your imagination.

Door-to-Door Cold Calling

If you can't afford any other way of reaching potential customers, put on a suit and start knocking on doors. Concentrate on a geographical area that you think contains a fair number of potential customers. This goes back to defining your product and its market.

When you're face to face with people who just might buy what you're selling, whether you've set the appointments up in advance over the phone or through the mail, or whether you've just knocked on their doors, don't try to blow them away with your high-powered spiel.

Listen to them.

Understand what they do.

Probe for their needs.

Then *translate* what you have to offer into *benefits* for them, into *solutions* for their problems.

We urge you not to sell "features." Proportional spacing with perfect right justification is a nifty feature, but if it does not somehow benefit your potential client, it's useless.

Features don't sell products.

Solutions do.

The U.S. Postal Service

The USPS offers substantial discounts on large mailings. Investigate third-class permits. There's an annual fee of \$40.00, and a one-time fee of \$40.00 for the right to print your own postage stamps. Since you save nine cents on the first ounce alone, you only need to mail 445 envelopes a year to break even on the annual fee—and not having to lick stamps repays itself in time savings on your first mailing.

In larger areas, your local post office will have someone on the payroll who deals with nothing but permit mailings. Talk to that person. You'll learn everything you need to know.

Ma Bell

Sooner or later you should list yourself in the Yellow Pages. Unlike a newspaper or a magazine or a piece of junk mail, people *keep* their phone books for at least a year, they keep them handy, and they have been trained by decades of advertising to "let their fingers do the walking."

It's easy to do. Call your phone company's administrative offices (listed right there in the front of the phone book) and say, "I'd like to put an ad in the Yellow Pages." The operator will connect you with the right department.

Now, the breakup of AT&T is causing the local phone companies' administrative procedures to diverge from the old AT&T norm, but in most areas you will have to take out business service on your telephone before you can get into the Yellow Pages. This will cost a little bit more each month. The person you're talking to will tell you how much more.

In most areas, business service automatically confers a free listing (name, address, and phone number) in your Yellow Pages directory. If people in your locality behave like other people across the country, this alone will generate enough extra business to pay the surcharge levied for business service.

Most phone companies offer two additional types of advertising: "in-column" and "display." The in-column ads are boxed lines of type right in the middle of the column; they're sold by the half-inch from one-half inch up to two and a half.

The display ads show up outside the columns, and offer you the chance to insert some graphics: your logo, for example, or a snapshot of your computer. These ads go in increments of one-sixteenth of a page, with one-sixteenth being the smallest.

Both types of ads are billed to you monthly, and the price of each varies according to the directory they're in. In

Connecticut, for example, the Hartford area directory is the most expensive. A one-half inch in-column ad there will run $21.60 a month (as of August 1, 1983), while a one-sixteenth-page display ad sets you back $71.20 a month.

Listings in other directories can be arranged for an additional fee. The person at the phone company will explain that to you, too.

Give serious consideration to listing yourself in the directory of areas abutting your own. Especially if you're doing any kind of training or consulting, where you're getting paid ridiculous sums of money for eight hours of work, one or two additional jobs a year will more than recoup the cost of the extra listings.

Clearly, an in-column ad doesn't have to generate a whole lot of business to pay for itself. Give Ma Bell a call. Her reps will help—and so will the ad.

The Good-Buddy Network

One final way of generating business for yourself is to staff your VSB with an army of sales representatives. It doesn't have to cost a thing.

We're talking word-of-mouth advertising here—the good-buddy network of people who know about you and recommend you to the people they come in contact with.

A satisfied customer is the best possible advertisement. Every time you sell a good or a service, make absolutely certain that the buyer gets several pieces of paper with your name and address and phone number on them—your card, your bill, your letterhead, your envelope. Your customers will find your business, but only if they remember how to find you.

Good buddies exist elsewhere, too.

Tell all your personal friends and acquaintances what you're doing. (Remember your mail-merge package?) Sooner or later each of them will encounter someone who is buying what you're selling. If they send some business your way, thank them—with a note for something small, maybe a dinner or a bottle or a bouquet for something really profitable. Make them feel appreciated, and they'll make you rich.

If you're selling your product to computer owners, go from store to store. Meet the people who sell the machines.

Tell them what you do, convince them you know how to do it, and explain how your doing it benefits them. (This might mean offering a finder's fee.) Then give each of them a few of your cards. Sooner or later, referrals will start to drift in.

Once you've set it up, the good-buddy network can keep you busy for a long, long time.

And that's what you want, yes?

Winning the Turf Wars

The only way to compete against established businesses is to be different. Charge less. Offer service at night and on weekends, whenever they don't. Most of the time, the new kid on the block can't go head-to-head with the biggest, toughest kids in town. Don't try. It hurts too much. . . .

How Much to Charge

For goods, you have to charge what they cost to make, a fair value for the time you put into making them, and a markup to cover the cost of handling and overhead (advertising, legal fees, utilities, etc.). If you discover that your prices are higher than those of comparable products, it's time to rethink your VSB.

For services, ask around and find out what others are charging. Charge less in the beginning than they do. There are a lot of cheapskates in the world who will hire you, rather than a long-established firm with a solid reputation, simply to save a few bucks. Without pointing a finger at anyone in particular, we feel safe in saying that people who spend their own money are more careful with it than are people who write checks off a multinational's account.

CHAPTER 5

The Soft Market

If you already have a solid background in computers and computer programming—or if you're willing to invest the time, money, and effort to learn—you can make anywhere from a few extra dollars to a few extra million by writing software.

Industry-wide, software sales reached six hundred million dollars in 1981, one billion dollars in 1982, and one and a half billion in 1983. On average, for every thousand dollars a consumer invests in hardware, he spends another three hundred on software within the next year. And there are hundreds of thousands of computer buyers out there.

All of that adds up to big money. For every Steve Wozniak (founder of Apple Computers) who's made a huge fortune in hardware design, there are a dozen slightly less immense fortunes made by the individuals and small companies writing the software for those computers.

With about forty thousand programs on retail shelves, it might seem that the market is crammed tight. Not true—in fact, software will reap huge profits over the next decade.

The two biggest assets a software designer can have are the imagination to see a software need and the persistence to figure out the best way of filling it. Each of the hundred-plus word-processing programs on the market, for instance, is trying to better its predecessors in capability, ease of use, affordability, or all of the above. Nobody has—yet—written the word-processing program that is *the* most capable, *the* easiest to use, and *the* most affordable. If somebody ever does, somebody else will sit down at a computer keyboard and try to better it.

New computers also create a need for new software—and new computers are coming on the market constantly. The IBM Personal Computer, with its then-new MS-DOS operating system, opened a market for CP/M programs adapted into a form that the IBM could use. It also stimulated the creation of brand-new programs, like Lotus 1-2-3™, which take advantage of the IBM's special capabilities—and which, as yet, have no corresponding program in CP/M or other operating systems.

While the rewards of software development can be great, the field is demanding. You will need most of the skills required for any other computer-based VSB—plus a knack for the art of developing software that other people will want (or better, *ache*) to buy.

Opportunity Doesn't Knock Once—It Knocks Three Times

Anyone who uses a computer is fair game for the software developer. Computers, you see, are useless lumps of plastic, metal, and silicon—without the instructions that make them perform. Those instructions fall into three broad categories:

General utility programs offer the greatest opportunity for huge financial rewards but are also, unsurprisingly, the most difficult field in which to make your mark. One of many examples of success is Microsoft, publisher of the MultiPlan spreadsheet program, which was founded by Bill Gates when he was eighteen. Company president Gates is now twenty-seven, and Microsoft's 1982 sales came to $34 million. When IBM was designing its Personal Computer, it asked Gates to write the operating system, MS-DOS.

Games are low-priced, high-volume items that demand a fanciful imagination. It isn't enough to come up with another variation on *Zaxxon* or *Frogger*; in order to succeed here, you have to create something new. And good.

Games come in two categories: graphics-oriented, and text-oriented. Graphics-based games make the crossover from video arcade to microcomputer with regularity. Text-oriented games, which take the form of a dialogue between the computer and the user, are limited to the microcomputer market.

Custom software is just that: programs tailored to the unique needs of a specific user. Often, these are adaptations of existing general utility programs. The markets are professionals, small businesses—and other VSBs.

Where to Learn

If the very thought of designing the next Perfect Writer™ or dBASE II™ fills you with excitement, but you know nothing at all of programming, find another VSB. Or spend a few years learning the skill. Programming, even in BASIC (a simple language), is not easy to master; most people don't have the patience to put in the effort necessary to become a professional programmer.

But don't get turned off. Programming is a good skill to have, even if you don't plan to go into software development. As a VSB operator, both your efficiency and your bankbook will profit from your ability to put together programs.

Half a dozen computer languages are used widely. BASIC, the easiest to learn, is limited by its simplicity, but it's a fine introduction to the world of programming. Computer retail outlets offer courses in BASIC, and in other languages. Workshops sponsored by universities, users' groups, and manufacturers are also good places to learn. If you are still in school, or don't mind returning, a college course is perhaps the best place to learn how to program—provided it teaches the principles of programming, not just one, or several, languages.

There are also hundreds of books available, covering all popular languages and most obscure ones. Check your local library or bookstore. Pick up one of the simpler BASIC primers, and see if the field still looks attractive. Teaching yourself exclusively from books is close to impossible and certain to be frustrating, but books are a good way to explore programming without spending a lot of money.

Finding the Market Space

Once you've decided that you enjoy programming for its own sake, and you've started to write your own sophisticated programs, you can begin to investigate the markets available to the VSB operator.

The software field is so tempting in part because the markets are so diverse. They range from the individual user—Phil next door, who can't figure out how to make his TRS-8Ø balance his checkbook—to the millions of people who either buy video games or play them at the neighborhood arcade or both.

But the market can also be confusing. Right now, it's in a state similar to that of the infant paperback publishing industry shortly after World War II: it's busy, and it's chaotic. Now that it's obvious there really are large profits in software, hundreds of new companies are springing up to carve out their pieces of the pie, while established companies are also getting into the field.

A new and growing force in software publishing is the print publisher. Harper and Row, for instance, sells a word-processing program called The Write Stuff. Other print publishers are pushing their way into the software markets and aiming primarily at the educational and entertainment segments. These generally low-cost programs can be retailed through the same outlets the publishers use to peddle their printware: the major bookstore chains like Waldenbooks and B. Dalton.

To help you sort your way through the maze, *Writer's Digest* is starting a series of *Programmer's Market* books to join their other guides for photographers and writers.

IBM Wants You—And They're Not Alone

Many of the larger hardware manufacturers actively encourage free-lance programmers to create new software for their machines.

Commodore in particular is receptive. The Commodore 64 and VIC-2Ø use a Texas Instruments microprocessor which does not run CP/M programs: programs written for the Commodore won't run on anything else, and only programs written exclusively for Commodore will run on their machines. They need more programs, for the more software written for the Commodore 64 and VIC-2Ø by enterprising VSB operators, the greater the appeal their machines will have for serious computer users.

Another market is the biggest computer company there ever was: IBM. IBM has an entire department devoted to nothing but looking at, evaluating, and buying so-called over-the-transom submissions.

A sure indicator of the vitality of the market is a recent series of ads from IBM. Run as two-page spreads in all the major magazines during the summer of 1983, the ads were nothing less than a solicitation of programs of all kinds for the IBM PC. (For information on how to submit, by the way, write IBM Personal Computer, External Submissions, Dept. 765PC, Armonk, NY 1Ø5Ø4.)

Be warned: the competition for the attention of these giants is *fierce.* Your work has to be very good to have a chance. If IBM does call and offer you a contract for your AutoGibberish word-processing program, you will need help. See **But I Can Do It Myself . . .** below.

The Art of Submission

The first step in submitting is to write.

As always, you should stick to what you know, at least at first. If you are an expert gamesman, you may well have the technical expertise to write a spreadsheet program—but you won't be as familiar with what is already available as you should be. There's no profit in reinventing the wheel. Know the market you want to write for.

You'll probably find that the best ideas for your own creations are sparked by the shortcomings of the programs you are using now—and your desire to go them one better. A lot of good programs have been written by someone who threw up his hands in frustration at the bugs in the program he was using and said, "I coulda written it better than *that* jerk."

By the time you've finished writing the program, you will probably already have a market in mind. If you're in doubt, take a look at companies that have been successful with similar types of programs. While MicroPro might be very interested in a new word-processing program—if it's very good—they would probably not be interested in a game written to run on the Atari 4ØØ, even if it were the best on the market.

Once you've picked the company, find the address in the latest *Programmer's Market,* or in the company's ads in the computer magazines.

So . . . you've got your program written and you've decided which company to give first crack at it; all you have to do is slip the disk into an envelope, mail it to the company's address, and wait for the offer to roll in, right?

Wrong. The only way to have a chance in the market is to be knowledgeable, personable—and *very* professional. Programming may be an art, but selling your program is a business. If you forget that, the businessman on the other side of the desk won't want to know you.

So act like a professional.

First: Find out who you're going to be dealing with—the person, not the company. Get the company on the phone and find out three things: the name of the person who handles external submissions, what format they want your program and your documentation in, and when you can expect a reply. Don't be pushy or hesitant; just calm and businesslike.

Second: Make your presentation look as clean and professional as possible. Use high-quality disks—and include a backup. Include also a printed copy of the program. Label everything with the name of the program and your own name, address, and telephone number. Don't forget documentation so the user will know how to operate your software. And don't forget to include return postage, in case they're too foolish to see that you've written the best program since VisiCalc.

Third: In a cover letter, tell them what the program is supposed to do and why it does it better than similar programs on the market. Include a very brief paragraph about any relevant professional credentials. Keep the letter short and businesslike. The company doesn't care if this is the first program you've ever submitted, or if you really need a lot of money for your sex-change operation, or if your mother thinks your program is just wonderful—all they care about is whether or not it's good. Don't distract them.

In all cases, remember that the market for over-the-transom software is new and still disorganized. As with paperbacks in the 1940s and 1950s, the procedures for submitting, purchasing, publishing, and distributing software are not well established. Have patience.

After: Worry. Will the company pirate your work? Will they lose it? If they do buy it, will they give you a fair shake?

The answer to all these questions is: you don't know. So take some precautions.

Piracy is not something to worry about. Your program (or anything else you write) is covered by the copyright law from the moment you put it on paper or disk—*if* you can prove that you wrote it.

So take an extra precaution. Register any program you're going to submit with the Copyright Office. Write to them for several copies of Form TX at: Register of Copyrights, Copyright Office, Library of Congress, Washington DC 20559. They'll send you back the form. Fill it out. Then slip the form, a printout of your program, and a check for the registration fee (ten dollars at present) into an envelope, stamp and address the envelope, throw the envelope in the mailbox, and sleep soundly. Once you've registered your program, you don't have to worry about proving that you wrote it.

That ten dollars may sound kind of stiff if you're going to be writing and registering a lot of programs. You should know that you can register a group of programs all at once with the same form—the whole group for that one ten-dollar fee. Write to the Copyright Office for details.

When the Postman Brings News—Good or Bad

If the company rejects your program, you'll be tempted to call them up and swear at them, or write them a letter telling them they've made a mistake, or just throw those disks into the trash.

Don't. Pick another company, and submit the program again.

And what if the news is good? What if Monstro Industries wants your AutoGibberish word-processing program and even includes a contract, complete with fine print, parties of the first part, and enough whereases to choke a horse?

If you are offered a contract, do *not* sit down immediately to sign it. Jump up and down with glee for a while, call all your friends and brag, chortle with pleasure, and have a sandwich.

Then get an agent, one who knows how to negotiate a software contract. If you haven't already bought *Programmer's Marketplace,* do so now. Turn to the section on agents, and pick one that looks good. If possible, call up one of the agent's clients and ask him or her how good the agent is.

Approach the agent in the same professional manner you did the software publisher. But use the phone for this; it'll save time. Get the agent himself or herself on the line (you've got an offer now; you don't have to deal with his secretary) and explain that you have been offered a contract and you would like him to negotiate it for you. In exchange, the agent will charge you 15 percent of any money you make off that contract (whether through royalties or flat payment). That's money well spent, especially for the novice.

"But I Can Do It Myself and Save Some Money"

Honest, you will need help.

Dealing with large companies isn't a job for an amateur. Negotiating a contract with a giant corporation is an art—and one you should be too busy to learn. A good agent will free you from some of your commercial concerns so you can spend more time programming.

The notion of agents representing software authors is a new thing. It's not surprising that some of the people doing it have been representing book authors for years.

New York City's Sterling Lord Agency is a literary agency that now represents software authors as well. Lord has represented clients in dealings with Texas Instruments and Coleco—and Bantam, Random House, and Simon and Schuster.

On the other hand, some agencies have been formed to represent software authors exclusively. The Software Company was formed when three agencies—Edward J. Acton, Sanford J. Greenburger Associates, and Moulter Associates—joined forces to market low-cost programs to bookstore chains like B. Dalton and Waldenbooks.

In any case, when IBM or TI or Commodore calls with an offer, say, "Thank you, I'll have my agent call you." And then rush right out and get one.

Going It on Your Own

Many VSB owners publish their own software, and many have, alas, gone out of business by doing so. Software publishing is as much an art as software writing. It isn't impossible, however, to write, duplicate, and market your own software, all by yourself. Companies specializing in games programs have found it easiest to pull themselves up by their own bootstraps in this fashion because customers are more likely to risk twenty to forty dollars for a game disk from an untried publisher than they are to fork over five hundred dollars for a word-processing program from the same source—no matter how good the word-processing program is.

Associations like the CP/M User's Group (1651 Third Avenue, New York, NY 10028) provide a large, readily accessible, but very idiosyncratic market, of sorts. For ten dollars CPMUG offers a catalogue of about one hundred disks of public domain software; they sell the disks, complete with working programs, for little more than blank disks cost.

Anyone can copy CPMUG programs, and either give the copies away or—*yes!*—sell them, either as-is, or tailored for an individual customer. In point of fact, the most popular—and in many people's opinion, the best—communications program, MODEM7, written by Ward Christensen, is available from CPMUG. If you know enough about software and hardware, you can make real money customizing MODEM7 for anyone with both a modem and a desire for a really good communications program. (See **Tailor-Made for Success,** below.)

There are advantages and drawbacks to going the public domain route. In the public domain there are games and utilities ready to run on many, many computers—but (1) the authors have no rights to the software, and (2) users are under no obligation to pay the authors one thin dime. Nevertheless, some do. If you write a program and let it fall into the public domain, be sure that it contains your name, address, and words to the effect of "Hi there. I wrote this. If you like it, I'm happy. As for me, I like money—can you take a hint?"

You're guaranteed not to make a fortune this way—but it can generate some publicity for you, as well as a little money, while you're working on more commercial material.

Good public domain programs *can* get you some attention. If Ward Christensen comes knocking on IBM's door, believe us, they'll answer. . . .

Tailor-Made for Success

The most proven market for the VSB operator is tailoring or designing software for individual users. Your market is huge: it's everyone you already know or can meet or can reach through advertising or word-of-mouth who either has or wants a microcomputer.

To do a lot of this, you must know quite a bit about hardware, as well as software. You might set yourself up as a consultant, offering clients a whole range of services. (For more on being a computer consultant, see Chapter 9, "Can a Piece of Your Mind Offer Them Peace of Mind?") Many times, it will be your knowledge of existing programs and how to use or alter them, not your ability to write new ones, that will be most useful to your client. And your bank account.

Jim Jones, a partner in the Columbus, Ohio–based Educational Computer Services, says his job is to allay clients' fear of computers and help them to avoid expensive mistakes. After only a few months in existence, ECS's two part-time operators had more work than they could handle. One of their first jobs was setting up a workstation for their lawyer's secretary, and tailoring existing word-processing, spreadsheet, and database management programs for the office's particular use.

Through their good-buddy network, Jones and partner Jerry McAfee can also write custom software.

Jones sees education as a major market that will grow in the future. Programs he writes or adapts include both "courseware" and classroom management software.

Computers will never replace teachers in the classroom, but courseware can supplement the teacher's skills, particularly in drills on such boring subjects—to the teacher; computers don't get bored—as multiplication tables. While a large array of courseware has already hit the market, the market is still growing.

Classroom management programs that keep track of attendance and grades, or even compute grading curves, also free the teacher from these routine and boring tasks.

Selling your program to a whole school system might be hard, but any teacher with a home computer and a loathing for those little red attendance and grade books should be easy pickings.

ECS has, so far, relied on word-of-mouth advertising to bring in clients. They haven't needed to pay for ads. Even charging thirty dollars an hour, the two partners have assignments lined up far into the future. They're doing well.

You can, too.

PART II

CHAPTER 6

You've Got It, They Want It: Services You Can Provide

Every small midwestern town has a Guy with a Truck. The truck is small and sturdy—usually a Willys—and it has a snowplow blade, and it spends its summers baking on a gravel lot with the junk cars behind the garage. Maybe by now it has a book value of only a few hundred dollars—it's old, and it's getting a little beat. But every winter that truck earns its owner a fortune.

He plows driveways with it. You figure twenty driveways per blizzard, times three or four blizzards per midwestern winter, times ten or twenty bucks for each job. That's sixteen hundred dollars each winter just for the big, paralyzing snowstorms. Add another sixteen hundred for routine snowfall, getting people out of ditches, jump-starting dead batteries, all the standard winter chores that guys with trucks do.

Thirty-two hundred dollars per winter is what the guy earns, minimum, and no one begrudges him a single cent of it. See, he's got the truck. And when you are stuck at midnight with a dead battery in a snowbank, you will pay almost anything to see, through the swirling snow, the wavering yellow high beams of a Willys coming to drag you out of the mess you've gotten your silly self into.

The guy is a capitalist, but around that small town he's a hero.

You can be like him. See, you've got the truck. In your case, the truck is a home computer. And if you work things right, your life from now on will be one long blizzard—of money.

You've got it: the skills, the equipment, and the desire to use them. They want it: the convenience, economy, and efficiency that your use of your equipment can provide.

Let's get *you* and *them* together, start a Very Small Business, and make money.

Here are some things you need to know, regardless of what kind of VSB you establish.

Space

Storage space. Working space. You need it. How much do you need? *No matter what your application, your computer and disk drives should run disks that are large enough for you to do and store your work on them.*

This may seem complicated to figure out, but it is not. The first thing you need to know is that one K equals 1Ø24 bytes. The second is that, while one byte really equals one typed character, other things take up space, too. So, when you are estimating space requirements, let one byte equal a little less than one typed character.

If you have 82K of storage on a disk, then you *could* get about 8Ø,ØØØ characters on it—but you shouldn't.

As a rule, for word processing, the space remaining on a disk should be more than twice the size of the largest file. This allows room for a backup file, which your machine may create automatically, and for "working files," which the system creates temporarily and within which it does its work.

Word-processing programs are rather more forgiving of "tight shoes" than are number-crunching programs, and data-processing programs are notorious for crashing if they get crowded. When they crash, they may take your data with them. A database for data-processing work should occupy no more than one-third of your storage disk.

In practical terms, this means that

a. 5¼″ disk drives are okay for short word-processing applications—letters, flyers, poems (except epics), and short stories. They will do for smaller number-crunching projects, too.

b. 8″ disks are much more convenient than 5¼″ for novels, theses, and other long word-processing jobs. They are necessary for data processing because the computer needs disk space to sort files. For big data-processing jobs, even 8″ disks may not be enough; you may want hard-disk storage to get the space you need for storing and manipulating large amounts of data. We'll tell you more about how to figure your data-processing space requirements in the section on data processing, below.

The other thing you need to know right away is how to figure out how much to charge.

How Much to Charge

We're assuming here that you want your system to pay for itself—at least.

Start by estimating the number of hours per week you want to devote to your VSB. Then estimate how long you expect your system to last. Add the cost of your system to the cost of the service contract over the system's estimated lifetime.

Let's say your system costs $6000, part of which is the cost of the service contract over five years—the estimated lifetime of your system—and you want to devote 20 hours per week to your VSB. Over five years, that's 2500 hours. $6000/2500 hours = $4.00 per hour to pay for the system.

Now estimate the amount of time you expect a particular job to take, multiply by $4.00 per hour, and add the cost of disks, supplies, the amount you expect to earn for your time, and your other overhead costs for the time spent on the job.

To figure overhead, you need to know what it costs to run your office per working hour, and what it costs to power your computer system. You might want to estimate what percentage of your home's floorspace is devoted to your office, and simply take that percentage of your utilities, phone, and so on as office overhead.

If you want to know how much it costs to run the computer, do it this way:

Amps (your computer spec sheet tells how many amps it runs on) times volts (your home is probably wired for 12Ø volts) equals watts. If a device uses 1ØØØ watts and you run it for an hour, then you've used a kilowatt-hour (kwh). For example, the Xerox 82Ø-II is a 5-amp system, and it runs on house current of 12Ø volts. Applying the formula, 5 amps × 12Ø volts = 6ØØ watts per hour, or .6 kwh. If your power costs 11 cents per kwh, running the 82Ø-II for an hour costs 6.6 cents.

Once you have figured out what you need to charge in order to make money on a job, *that's what you charge.* You may find that your prices are much higher than those of comparable businesses in your area. Resist the temptation to match their prices, unless you can reduce your costs. You may decide to charge less for your time than you had planned, but remember that you are in this to make money, not to give your time away.

Remember, too, that larger businesses can afford to lose money on some jobs in order to get customers for other, more lucrative work. You are not a larger business. There are some areas in which you will not be able to compete with the big boys on the block. If you can't make money on one VSB, don't beat your head against the wall—start another that *does* make money. Your honor is not at stake here, but your bankroll is.

Fattening That Bankroll

Okay—what *can* you do to make money with your home computer?

The services you can provide to others with your home

computer fall fairly neatly into three categories: word processing, number processing, and data processing.

In the Beginning Is The Word

Word-processing services fall into two subcategories: you can process your own words, or the words of others. Either way, the *product* is the same: clean, readable, correctly formatted copy—of a book, thesis, form letter, legal document, or whatever text you or your customer may need. Let's talk first about working for others; a little further on, we'll discuss working—and writing—for yourself.

Typing for Others

A word-processing service is the same as an old-fashioned typing service, except that the work is easier and more lucrative.

JOBS

What kinds of jobs can you get? Jobs like these:

Straight typing. You simply type what the customer gives you to type, in the format the customer desires.

1. The market: You can type theses, term papers, reports, monographs, books, grant proposals, journal articles—all the reams and reams of writing that businesspeople, academics, students, writers, and others need typed.

2. The price: Check your area for the going rate. It's about $1.50 per page in our locality, more for statistical typing (pages of numbers), single-spacing, or other special formats.

3. Caveats: The work can be tedious, yet you must be careful about details. Make sure the customer states exactly what is wanted, make sure you hear correctly, and make sure you do it that way. Remember that some typing businesses are seasonal; theses are a good example. All the students will want theirs done in April, unless you persuade them to schedule early and/or in advance (see **When to Say No,** below).

4. A related service: You might wish to sell the finished disk to your customer, too. If you've got the disk stored away, your customer can get a cheap rewrite and you'll be more likely to get a return customer.

5. Required equipment: Word-processing software,

disks, and disk drives large enough to store documents of the size you wish to type. For this and all the other jobs described in this chapter, you need hardware that will run software and disks of the type and size appropriate for the job (see **Space,** above). Also: a letter-quality printer with tractor-feed attachment for form-feed paper, and (this may be optional) memory buffer for typing one project while printing another.

Typing boiler-plate documents. Boiler-plate documents are standard forms, such as contracts or insurance forms, into which variable information must be inserted.

1. *The market:* Attorneys, physicians, insurance agents, accountants, and others whose jobs involve filling out the same forms over and over.

2. *The price:* Charge a "straight typing" rate to get the forms onto your disks, and for the information you insert into the forms. Charge a flat fee for each filled-in form you generate. To decide on the typing rate and the flat fee, call a few local word-processing services in your area and ask what they charge for comparable work. Your fee should be competitive, and it should be less than the customer is already paying.

3. *Caveats:* When you run a boiler-plate document service, you must be available during business hours to do the work, sometimes on short notice. You must arrange for a reliable replacement if you are away. Remember, too, that the information you handle may be interesting—but it is confidential.

4. *Related service:* If you get a lot of assignments from one business office, you might lease that office a modem and printer. Then you can get information and deliver the finished forms without leaving *your* office.

5. *Required equipment:* Word-processing software that includes some sort of merge-print feature, a letter-quality printer with a tractor feed, and plenty of disk space for storing boiler-plate document forms. For this and all the other jobs described in this chapter, you need hardware that will run software and disks of the type and size appropriate for the job (see **Space,** above). Again, you may want a memory buffer. Modems are convenient but not necessary right away.

Producing camera-ready copy. You can simply type columns of copy, sized correctly for the customer's newsletter or small magazine format. Or you can offer a package deal: they supply the words, and you do everything else—typing, layout, securing artwork—the entire production.

1. *The market:* All kinds of social, fraternal, and professional organizations produce newsletters for their members.

2. *The price:* For typing and formatting, charge your straight typing rate. For a package deal, charge a package price that includes your costs, overhead, and an hourly rate for your time, plus the hourly rate for your computer (see above, **How Much to Charge**).

3. *Caveats:* Layout (the process of positioning material on a page) looks idiotically simple. It is in fact moderately difficult for the experienced, and devilishly hard for the novice. Start small—with a flyer, say. Don't offer to secure artwork unless you know artists who can supply it, and don't forget to figure the cost of it into the price you charge.

4. *Related service:* You can offer to mass-mail the newsletter, becoming, in effect, a publisher. For information about small publishing, write to COSMEP, The Coalition of Small Press Editors and Publishers, Box 7Ø3, San Francisco, CA 941Ø1. Visit the post office to get information about mass-mailing regulations.

5. *Required equipment:* Word-processing software with merge-print feature; letter-quality printer with tractor feed. For this and all the other jobs described in this chapter, you need hardware that will run software and disks of the type and size appropriate for the job (see **Space,** above). For publishers: art supplies for layout, database management software for managing subscription lists, form-feed labels for mailing newsletters.

Resume service. A printed resume looks ostentatious, while a photocopied one looks just a bit tacky. What's really wanted is an original sheet, perfectly typed with a carbon ribbon and correctly formatted on good bond paper.

1. *The market:* Schools will provide you with customers for this service. You may get referrals from employment agencies, too. Don't neglect organizations such as the League of Women Voters, the National Association of Uni-

versity Women, sheltered workshops for the handicapped, fraternal and professional organizations, and local veterans' groups.

2. The price: Call a few local resume-preparing services to get an idea of the going price in your area. Your price should be comparable or a little less when you start out—although it shouldn't be lower than is worth your while (see **How Much to Charge,** above).

3. Caveats: Resumes must be perfect. Proofread carefully. If you think a change is required, check it out—tactfully—with the customer before delivering the finished resume.

4. Related service: Create a database of the names and addresses of job-hunters (with their permission, of course). Then offer a personalized form-letter service to firms who might advertise to job-hunters.

5. Required equipment: Word-processing software; letter-quality printer. For this and all the other jobs described in this chapter, you need hardware that will run software and disks of the type and size appropriate for the job (see **Space,** above).

Typing for Yourself

Writing for yourself—*creative* writing, as it is loosely called—is, as everyone knows, just sheer, unrelenting, nonstop fun. Yep, it's a laugh a minute around *our* office, we can tell you . . . uh, where were we?

Oh, yes—writing.

Look about you. The printed word is everywhere. It's on billboards and in reports and on the backs of cereal boxes. It's in instruction books and fortune cookies and on the fronts of T-shirts. There are more words around than you can shake a stick at, and every one of those words has one thing in common:

Somebody had to write it.

Press releases. Publicity write-ups. Personalized childrens' books and letters from Santa. Family histories for annual gatherings, and local histories for neighborhood organizations. The blurbs that run on the insides and backs of book jackets. Annual reports to stockholders. Church bulletins. Informational packages for everything from condominiums to vacation tours.

Pick something that you understand, and write about it.

JOBS

Blurb writing. Jacket copy, especially for texts and other special-market books, may be written by free-lancers with expertise in the book's subject. Large publishers employ people for this chore, but the smaller houses often farm it out.

1. The market: Small publishers. Some won't call themselves publishers; they may list themselves in the Yellow Pages as Axolotl Press, for example. If you have special knowledge, go for houses that publish books on your subject. But don't sell yourself short: lots of people have knowledge, but not many can write.

2. The price: This will vary greatly. Try to find someone with whom you will not be in competition, but who knows the local market. Then—ask. Anywhere from $5Ø to $1ØØ is reasonable, although you may have to do one or two projects for free, to show that you can.

3. Caveats: Jacket copy must conform to the publisher's style. Familiarize yourself with the copy on other books from the house for which you wish to work. To write copy for texts and other specialized books, you must know the subject and be able to place the book in context with other works of its kind.

4. Related service: If you know how to prepare an index, you can offer a free-lance indexing service to professional and university presses (see **Indexing,** below).

5. Required equipment: Word-processing software for text and correspondence; database management software for sorting index entries; letter-quality printer. For this and all the other jobs described in this chapter, you need hardware that will run software and disks of the type and size appropriate for the job (see **Space,** above). You may also need a tractor feed and memory buffer.

Annual reports. Every publicly held corporation—that is, every company that offers shares for sale—is required by law to produce an annual report for shareholders. Large businesses employ people to write and produce these, but small businesses can't afford to.

1. The market: Local publicly held corporations. Local stockbrokers will be able to identify these businesses for you, or they may be listed in your newspaper.

2. The price: $10 per hour or more for brief reports. If the report must meet Securities and Exchange Commission requirements, charge more. Consult a CPA (and pay for the consultation—it's worth it) to learn what is being charged by others.

3. Caveats: You must be a CPA in order to produce some kinds of annual reports. Even if you don't need to be certified, you will need business knowledge in order to write these correctly.

4. Related service: Offer your report-writing service to CPAs. They dig out the figures and do the calculations; you compose the report. You might also produce camera-ready copy for your own or for others' already-written reports, along the small-publishing lines suggested in the word-processing section, above.

5. Required equipment: You'll need spreadsheet and database management software if you do any number-crunching yourself. For this and all the other jobs described in this chapter, you need hardware that will run software and disks of the type and size appropriate for the job (see **Space,** above). For composing and formatting reports you need word-processing software, a letter-quality printer with tractor-feed attachment, and perhaps a memory buffer.

Personalized "info-stories" for children. Write a personalized story for a child, and include the child's dog, blanket, grandparents, his favorite toys, and his playmates. Include also his name, address, phone number, and the full name of a trusted neighbor.

The child, of course, will make you read it again and again, and probably memorize every word—including his name and address, phone number, and the name of the neighbor.

Sneaky, hey? Next time the child wanders off in the shopping mall, you'll be glad you did it—and you'll probably be able to sell personalized "info-stories" to the parents of the child's playmates, as well.

1. The market: Friends and relatives of small children.

2. The price: Your hourly rate and overhead multiplied by the number of hours you spend, plus your costs to produce the book, all divided by the number of copies you expect to sell.

3. Caveats: You need to be familiar with the vocabulary that can be understood by a small child. The story must be interesting enough to hold the child's attention. And if little Sally's dog is named Spat, don't call him Spot.

4. Related service: If you can write for children, why not write for children? Collaborate with an artist, and submit your book to publishers of children's books.

5. Required equipment: Word-processing software with merge-print feature; letter-quality printer with tractor feed. For this and all the other jobs described in this chapter, you need hardware that will run software and disks of the type and size appropriate for the job (see **Space,** above).

These are just a few of the ways you can make money on your own writing. Look around. Behind nearly every printed word, you can find that elusive but common species, the paying customer.

Perhaps, though, you're not really interested in words. Perhaps numbers are your friends, your familiars, your stock-in-trade. Perhaps you know a secret:

Numbers Are Not Beasts

Number-crunching applications (as opposed to data processing, which is discussed below) are those that require you and your computer to perform calculations.

JOBS

Number-crunching service.

1. The market: Students, sales reps, engineers, contractors, insurance agents, accountants, and anyone who must manipulate numbers quickly and accurately. This is an especially good VSB for you if you are a student yourself—your customers are all around you.

2. The price: See **How Much to Charge,** above.

3. Caveats: You must learn to use the spreadsheet software well before you can offer this service. Although the computer does the actual calculating for you, it helps to have some mathematical ability. You shouldn't be stupidly plugging numbers into equations; if you don't understand what you're doing, you won't notice your own errors.

4. A related service: If you have math ability and find that you enjoy and are good at number crunching, you might want to move on into database management—see below.

5. Required equipment: Word-processing software for text that may be included in projects; calculator spreadsheet software; plenty of disk storage. For this and all the other jobs described in this chapter, you need hardware that will run software and disks of the type and size appropriate for the job (see **Space,** above). A dot-matrix printer *might* be adequate for number-crunching work. Also, get a copy of Texas Instruments' *Calculator Decision-Making Handbook.*

Biorhythms. A big market still exists for biorhythm calculations, which are thought to describe physical, emotional, and intellectual cycles in human beings. They are calculated from the moment of an individual's birth. You can buy a book on how to do it (see Part IV, *Sources*).

1. The market: You may calculate for individuals, or sell a column to your local newspaper or to periodicals.

2. The price: Negotiable. You don't tell newspapers and periodicals what they will pay; they tell you. For individuals, see **How Much to Charge**, above.

3. Caveats: You'll need at least a rudimentary understanding of how to program in BASIC. You can get a biorhythm-calculation program from one of the many BASIC "recipe books" on the market, but you'll still have to get the program up and running on your computer. Express yourself in positive terms; for example, if the numbers predict "low points," you might recommend patience and expectation of better days to come.

4. Related service: Write a story or an article, humorous or not, slanted toward a market with which you are already familiar. For example, you might calculate biorhythms for fictional mothers of small children, and show how the predictions worked out in practice.

5. Required equipment: You'll need a database management program for this, as well as enough disk space to do the work and store it. For this and all the other jobs described in this chapter, you need hardware that will run software and disks of the type and size appropriate for the job (see **Space,** above). Dot-matrix printers may be good enough to calculate biorhythms for individuals; for selling to publications, you'll want double-dot-matrix, at least. Some publications won't even read dot-matrix-produced submissions.

Horoscopes. Horoscopes are somewhat more complicated to calculate than biorhythms, and for them you will have to write a program.

1. *The market:* Individuals and publications. Again, you might slant your work toward a group with which you are already familiar.

2. *The price:* As for biorhythms, the price depends on your market. See **How Much to Charge,** above.

3. *Caveats:* You can't cast horoscopes unless you know how. You'll need to know how to write programs, too, and how to run a database management program.

4. *Related service:* Collaborate with an artist, and create computerized horoscope charts with an attractive, "high-tech" appearance. If you write an original horoscope-casting program (not an alteration of a copyrighted database management program), you may be able to sell that, too (see chapter 5, "The Soft Market").

5. *Required equipment:* A database management software package that can be customized to write the horoscope-casting program, and plenty of disk storage space. For this and all the other jobs described in this chapter, you need hardware that will run software and disks of the type and size appropriate for the job (see **Space,** above). You'll need word-processing software for text. A dot-matrix printer may be good enough, but the printout will have a most "unmystical" appearance. For publication, you'll probably need a letter-quality printer.

Product pricing. Other VSB operators may need help in deciding what to charge for their goods or services. You can help them calculate their prices. Of course, you'll first need to know how to calculate prices (see **How Much to Charge,** above).

1. *The market:* Anyone who charges for goods or services.

2. *The price:* See **How Much to Charge.**

3. *Caveats:* To work in this area, you will need general business knowledge and preferably some experience, too. You'll need to know a lot about each individual customer's business, and about what others in comparable businesses are charging. Several sessions at the customer's workplace may be required to familiarize yourself with all the factors affecting your customer's prices. You may need to do some reading and research on your own, as well.

4. *A related service:* If you enjoy and are good at pricing, and you have the required business knowledge and experience, you might want to offer database management services to businesses, too (see **Database Management,** below).

5. *Required equipment:* Calculator spreadsheet and database management software, and plenty of disk storage space. For this and all the other jobs described in this chapter, you need hardware that will run software and disks of the type and size appropriate for the job (see **Space,** above). A dot-matrix printer is probably fine for pricing.

Database Management

As soon as we get into pricing, we're really out of the pure numbers realm. The numbers are now attached to real objects, and those objects have names. Not only do we want to count the objects, we want to make lists of them, sort the lists in various ways, and do calculations that give us more information about them.

Can you keep books? Can you manage money, property, expense accounts, investments, sports-league scores, taxes, profit-and-loss statements—are you confident handling numbers? Lots of people aren't. That's why they will pay you to do it for them, especially since you can do it better with your home computer.

Here let us point out that if you are a bookkeeper or CPA, your home computer will let you do your work faster and more accurately. There are software packages for payroll, accounts payable, accounts receivable, general ledger, tax accounting, investment management, cash flow, inventory, and every conceivable accounting chore. Using them will simplify the bookkeeper's or CPA's life immensely.

We aren't going to list here all the jobs a CPA can do. If you're not already familiar with them, you probably aren't equipped to attempt them. If you don't understand how businesses work, if you can't walk into a business establishment and speak intelligently about solving the proprietor's problems with your service, then business database management is not for you. The computer won't give you business acumen that you do not already possess. On the other hand, special knowledge that you do have may open specialized areas of database management to you (see **Jobs,** below).

No matter what sort of database management service you establish, you will need to calculate space requirements. As we mentioned above, you need *plenty* of space.

Space for Your Database—How Much?

Here's how to figure out how much space a job will require.

Let us say that you are managing inventory for Tom's Surplus Store. (Remember, this is just an example. Estimating space requirements for nonbusiness database management works the same way.) You will make a *record* for each item of stock Tom carries. Within that record, you will fill in *fields:* Item, Supplier, Price, Stock #, Stock Location, Amount on Hand, and Date of Last Order, for instance. That's seven *fields.*

Now, how many *characters* are in each field? (You won't know until you make a sample record. You can do this with pencil and paper.) Add up the total number of *characters* in all the fields. That's the number of *characters* in a *record.*

Now, how many items of inventory will you manage for Tom? That's the number of *records* you are going to write. Multiply the number of *characters* in one *record* by the number of *records* you are going to keep. The result is the number of characters your whole database will require. You need at least three times that much space on your disk. Buy disk drives and disks accordingly. If you already own your system, don't take jobs that are too big for your working and storage capacities.

JOBS

As we mentioned above, bookkeepers and CPAs can streamline their work with database management systems. But there are other jobs for database managers, too.

Connoisseur consultant. If you know a lot about wines, art, antique cars, wooden boats, or other collectibles, you might create a database containing information about them.

1. The market: Buyers and sellers of all kinds of rarities will want the information you have collected and organized, especially if your database is the most complete. Periodicals devoted to your special interest may purchase articles or columns containing recent prices at auction, ownership histories, even trivia contests.

2. The price: As mentioned above, you don't charge periodicals for your work; they decide how much they will pay. If you are creating and maintaining a database for an individual, see **How Much to Charge,** above.

3. Caveats: Choose a subject that is not too esoteric to be of interest to anyone else, but which has not already been "worked over" by some other researcher. Define your topic narrowly at first, so that you may be thorough.

4. Related service: Start a newsletter containing the results of your own research and the work of others. You might sell this to special-interest groups, or organize a new group.

5. Required equipment: Database management software; word-processing software for correspondence and newsletters. A dot-matrix printer is good enough for data printout, but you'll want letter quality for work that is to be published. Eight-inch disks may be large enough, but for large collections of data you may need hard-disk storage. For this and all the other jobs described in this chapter, you need hardware that will run software and disks of the type and size appropriate for the job (see **Space,** above).

Indexing. Many small publishers employ free-lance indexers who arrange alphabetical lists of topics in books and periodicals, along with their page numbers, for easy reference.

1. The market: Publishers of texts, reference books, and general nonfiction, as well as publishers of periodicals.

2. The price: Varies among publishers. Once you are known in the field, it may become negotiable.

3. Caveats: You need to be reasonably well versed in the topic of the book or periodical you index, so that your index will make sense to readers. Indexing is a craft; you can learn the basics from books, but doing it well takes some practice. Start with small projects in an area with which you are familiar.

4. Required equipment: You'll need database management software for sorting index listings; word-processing software for correspondence and other text; and a letter-quality printer with tractor-feed attachment. For this and all the other jobs described in this chapter, you need hardware that will run software and disks of the type and size appropriate for the job (see **Space,** above).

Bibliographies. A bibliography of your area of special expertise is another project for a database, especially if your knowledge is uncommon.

1. The market: Special-interest periodicals, writers, researchers, students.

2. The price: Depends on the market. Periodicals will set their own prices. For individuals, see **How Much to Charge,** above.

3. Caveats: In order to be salable, a bibliography must be useful. Define your topic carefully: if it is too narrow, it will be of interest only to yourself; too general, it will be a clumsy research tool.

4. Related service: Once you have compiled a bibliography, you might go on to do the research yourself, and write books and articles on your topic.

5. Required equipment: Database management software for sorting entries; word-processing software for correspondence, magazine articles, and books. For this and all the other jobs described in this chapter, you need hardware that will run software and disks of the type and size appropriate for the job (see **Space,** above). A dot-matrix printer will be good enough to generate reports, but if you intend to submit material for publication, you will need a letter-quality printer, and you may need a tractor-feed attachment.

On-line information sources such as The Source, as well as more specialized information services, may be necessary to compile thorough bibliographies. Even if you don't absolutely need them, on-line information services will save you a great deal of time. If you decide they are worth your investment, you will need a modem, too.

Mailing lists. You can create and maintain lists for advertising and other mailing purposes with your computer and a database management system, and you can print mailing labels sorted in any order you wish.

1. The market: Small publications and newsletters, businesses, advertising agencies, public relations companies, charities, clubs, political causes.

2. The price: See **How Much to Charge,** above.

3. Caveats: If you do the mailing for a customer, be sure to charge for this service as well, and be sure that you are thoroughly familiar with postal regulations regarding mass mailing. Visit your post office for a chat with the person whose job it is to familiarize you with the regulations. Make friends with this person if you can; you will find a good working relationship with the U.S. Postal Service invaluable to you.

4. A related service: You can type, format, and print the material being mailed by the customer, personalizing each piece if that is desired. You and the organizations whose lists you are maintaining may also earn money by renting the mailing lists to companies who wish to advertise in your community.

5. Required equipment: Word-processing software with a merge-print option, for text and correspondence; database management software for creating and sorting lists. For this and all the other jobs described in this chapter, you need hardware that will run software and disks of the type and size appropriate for the job (see **Space,** above). You will need a dot-matrix or letter-quality printer, depending on the needs of your customers; you will need also a tractor-feed attachment for printing items to be mailed, and for printing the mailing labels themselves.

When to Say No

One of the most important things to know about your Very Small Business, whatever it may be, is that you don't have to take every job that comes along. There will be times when you must turn down business. You should say no, when

1. You don't have the knowledge the job requires, and you don't have the time, interest, or ability to acquire the knowledge;

2. You don't have the time to do the job without sacrificing things you don't want to sacrifice—such as your spouse, your kids, your sleep, or your other professional commitments;

3. You don't have the equipment required for the job (hardware, software, or whatever) and you can't justify buying it because you won't get enough use out of it to make it pay for itself; or

4. You don't want to work for this particular customer because you think the customer won't pay, or is impossible to satisfy, or is a shady character, or because you have a funny feeling you can't ignore and the feeling says "Don't."

When you do turn down a job, explain to the customer that you are saying no for the customer's own good. Refer the customer to someone who can do the job, if you know someone. Your honesty will make the customer happy. Your referral will make the person who gets the job happy. And you will be happy, since the job wasn't right for you in the first place.

There is, on the other hand, one instance in which you should probably take a job even though you are reluctant. That is the instance in which the job is unusually challenging—more so than you are accustomed to. You have the knowledge, time, and equipment, and the customer seems fine—but you're scared. You know you can do the job—it's just a little bigger, a little more complicated, just a bit more demanding of your knowledge, talent, and skills than your previous assignments have been.

That's the job you *want*—whether you know it or not.

It's the job that will stretch you and force you and your VSB to grow. It's the one that will increase your pride, your self-confidence, and your profits—the one that will prove to you once and for all that You Can Do It.

You can do it. Take your time. Don't jump into anything, and don't start big if you feel like starting small. Let the suggestions in this chapter spur your imagination and your initiative. Think about what you know well and about what you like to do. Then decide on the one service that you are going to provide, leaving all thought of diversification for later on.

Now, prepare carefully. Prepare your workplace, your work schedule, your equipment and supplies. Make your ground rules regarding which jobs you will take, and what you will charge for them. Assemble a plan for attracting customers, and pump up your self-confidence.

You can do it. Just *do it.* Plan carefully, prepare carefully, and work carefully. Have some old-fashioned faith in yourself. Do your best, and believe that your best will be good enough. Most likely it will.

If you fail, pick yourself up and try again, perhaps at some other sort of VSB. Learn from the experience, and don't kick yourself too hard. After all, you're not running Chrysler Corporation—just a Very Small Business.

CHAPTER 7

Do You Know What What You Know Is Worth?

Training

If you've been thinking of providing electronic services to non-computer owners, it may dishearten you to realize that, at its present rate of annual growth, the computer industry will have sold every citizen of the United States at least one PC by the end of 1985. (And that's one reason our publishers are paying us to write *The Electronic Money Machine*—they realize just how rapidly this market is expanding.)

But don't worry about having no market for your VSB. Were the industry to sustain that sort of growth, it would have to ship 350,000,000 personal computers in 1986 alone. We'd all be up to our ASCIIs in hardware. Not something to fret about any time soon.

A more realistic estimate for 1986 predicts that Americans will spend some fourteen billion dollars on personal computers and related equipment.

Three billion of that will go for computer education.

This, for you, is the nice part of it. Most citizens of the United States haven't the foggiest idea of how to run a personal computer. Or what to do with one if they have one. (And that's another reason why *The Electronic Money Machine* has found its way into your hands—we're here to tell you the possibilities inherent in your machine.)

See, with your knowledge and experience, you can teach.

Teach, huh? That conjures up the image of a nervous, underpaid individual confronting a roomful of high school students, all the while wishing for a chair, a whip, and a gun.

Clear *that* image right out of your head. Replace it with this one:

Two hundred dollars per day. Minimum. Nice image, eh?

You must understand three things:

Most people who design computers and who write programs aren't on speaking terms with the English language. The reference manuals they produce are about as useful to the average PC buyer as a copy of the Bible in the original Hebrew is to the average churchgoer.

Further, the profit margin on a two- or three-thousand-dollar machine is fairly low, and the dealer can't afford to provide a lot of free training and/or support. This leads to a terrible frustration in those who have just plonked down several thousands of dollars for a computer: they can't figure out how to order it to do what it's supposed to, and no one has time to tell them.

Finally, a lot of people are terrified just by the word "computer"—especially if a "computer error" has erased their bank balance or landed them in an insane hassle with a government agency which insists they died years ago. When these people's employers buy microcomputers for them to work on, they need a lot of hand-holding. The person who can allay their fears is a walking gold mine.

That's where you come in. You are the middleman, the

interface, the grease on the gears. You enable the buyer to run what the designer has created, and you make things as smooth as possible for both parties.

So how do you start?

To begin with, you start here as you've started elsewhere: by defining your skills.

Foremost among them must be the ability to teach. You must be able to explain what you know in language that's clear *not only to you* but also to the person who's listening to you.

If you can't talk about computers except in RAMs, ROMs, picoseconds, head step rates, semi-disks, system calls, and all that jargon, the odds are excellent that you will only fluster the secretaries whose bosses are willing to pay for personalized instruction.

If, on the other hand, you can hold up a floppy and say, "We call this a floppy disk. It's like a cassette in a tape recorder. It's where everything you type will be stored. This thing here is the disk drive. It works a lot like a cassette recorder. Which means you have to keep your fingers and your cookie crumbs off this shiny stuff you see on the disk. . . ." If you can do that, and enjoy it because you're making the most marvelous machine ever given to the human brain comprehensible to someone who's probably scared silly of it, then maybe you've got what it takes to be a computer trainer.

Maybe. Because you also need patience. Lots and lots and *lots* of it. Fair warning: you are going to have to deal with people who ask—each of them for the eighty-third time—"Why did it erase my disk when I turned it off?" And you must explain why as patiently as possible, as clearly as possible; because on the one hand, *that* person's work got trashed, not yours, and on the other hand, you're getting paid to be patient.

So you need patience. You need the ability to describe high-tech electronics in low-tech basic English.

And you need two kinds of expertise: hardware and software.

Hardware

Generally speaking, hardware expertise is not crucial. The people who want to know how the hardware *really* works won't be paying you to teach them; they'll futz around with it themselves, or they'll go to electronics school. Everybody else will know that there are zillions of different machines on the market, and they won't expect you to be 1ØØ percent knowledgeable on every facet of every machine. You don't insist that a driving instructor know where the solenoid is on every model of automobile, do you?

What you do expect of driving instructors—and what your customers will demand of you—is the ability to get the machine started.

For you, this means being able to find the on/off switch. (Given that computer manufacturers compete to see who can best hide it, that's not as dumb as it sounds.) You must know how to load every machine you attempt to train on, how to get it to output to its printer, and how to skim through the manual, extracting both the essentials and some of the niceties.

Don't misunderstand: we aren't suggesting that it's okay to be completely ignorant of the various sorts of hardware floating around. It's not. You should be familiar with four or five of the most popular systems, and you should be able to cope with all the rest after a few private minutes with the system reference manual.

Three product lines with which we urge you to become acquainted—not because they're tops, but because you're so likely to find customers who own them—are IBM, Apple, and Radio Shack. Timex/Sinclair, Commodore (the VIC line), Texas Instruments, Atari, and Coleco may sell more units, but let's face it, who's going to pay $2ØØ to learn how to run a $79 machine? Other lines to watch for include DEC, Victor, Osborne, KayPro, and Morrow.

And you should know one system—your own—inside and out. The similarities among microcomputers are so great that almost any of them will do most of what most of the rest will do—and if you know *exactly* how to do it on your own machine, figuring out how to do it on a foreign system will be a lot easier.

Besides which, it can only help to establish a reputation as the local expert on your model computer. You'll be surprised how many calls you'll get from people who say,

"Hey, I hear you've got the same system I'm thinking of buying, and I was wondering . . ."

Software

You thought there were a lot of *systems* around? At last count some *forty thousand* software packages had hit the marketplace, and better than a thousand new programs a month are fighting for shelf space.

Clearly, it's impossible—not to mention impractical—for you to become expert at more than a few of them. Fortunately, if you're looking to earn money teaching, you don't need to.

What you must do is master one or several of the most popular packages in one or more of the following categories:

Operating systems. CP/M in all its versions is probably the most popular. MS-DOS is catching up quickly, primarily because it's what the IBM PC uses. TRSDOS™ is Radio Shack's; AppleDOS™ is Apple's. Unix is gathering devotees, too.

Word Processing. WordStar is the overall sales leader, and if you know it you'll find lots of people who want to learn it. Perfect Writer and Easy Writer™ are right up there, as are Scripsit™, Select, and AppleWriter.

Spreadsheets. VisiCalc opened the doors for a host of "VisiClones," but is still the all-time best seller. SuperCalc is neat, and lately MultiPlan has been selling well. Lotus 1-2-3 is winning a reputation for itself.

Database management systems. dBase II™ from Ashton-Tate is undoubtedly the most widely used package of all, but by the time this book hits print, something will surely have superseded it.

Specialized packages. These include accounting packages specifically designed for certain professions (such as Legal Tender™ and The Professional™); general ledger type programs (BOSS™, for example); engineering packages; and thousands upon thousands of others. Advice: if you're not familiar with the profession itself, don't try to get into this area.

Languages. Most programming languages are available in versions specifically designed for microcomputers. These include most variants of BASIC (the most widely known language, though hardly the most useful); CBASIC™, FORTRAN, COBOL, PASCAL. . . . The list goes on and on. Recommendation: if you already know a language, get good at it, become familiar with the varietals available, and branch out from there.

Which categories should you specialize in? And which specific programs within those categories should you master? Well, that depends entirely on who you think your market is (for how to find it, see Part I, chapter 4), and how much work you want or need. The more you know, the more you can teach.

But first decide whether you want to work for yourself, or for someone else.

If you want to work for someone else, your market consists of every computer-training institution in your area, from high schools and colleges through computer stores and specialized "academies of computer education."

By the way, working for someone else does *not* necessarily mean wearing a suit and tie to an office for eight hours a day, five days a week. Many places that offer computer training actually prefer to hire free-lance trainers for specific jobs (say a one-night-a-week course in word processing) because there's a lot less paperwork involved (no withholding, no social security, no workmen's comp), and because they pay you only for time that produces income for them.

If you just want to earn enough to pay for the care and feeding of your own computer, this might be the best way. Once you've found an employer or two, all you have to do is show up on time and teach well. You don't have to hunt for students, maintain a classroom full of expensive equipment, or find unknown addresses in driving rainstorms. Your "employer" does all of that.

Teaching one two-hour class every week, at $2Ø an hour, yields you $2Ø8Ø in one year—$1Ø,4ØØ over the five-year depreciable life-span of your system. Not a bad return on your initial investment and a mere 1.7 percent of your waking hours. . . . Plus, if you're any good, you're guaranteed to get an extra job now and then from a student who wants to go farther or deeper than the course did. For that you can ask $30 an hour, easily.

If you work for yourself, your market consists of everyone in your area who needs training on a personal computer. Finding them won't be as easy as letting someone else do it for you, but the payoff to you is much, much better.

You can train at their place or at yours; you can teach one student at a time or a whole class of them—and it's your choice!

In the beginning, at least, offering customer-site training is probably the best way to go. It calls for a minimum investment on your part—clean clothes and some form of transportation (buses are perfectly acceptable). You don't need to worry about keeping your office clean and your machines running; you don't have the problem of teaching on systems different from the customers'. This is truly a VSB you can run from a corner of your living room.

Of course, if you do it often enough, you'll probably have a very nice living room: the first time out you can ask (and get) $15 an hour, then bump that up to $25 an hour by the fifth or sixth time you've done it.

The director of training at a local computer store charges for customer-site training on the following basis: $35 per hour for the first three students, and an additional $10 per hour for every student thereafter. One company hired her to train eleven people; she taught for eight hours and billed them $105 per hour—$840 for the day.

That's high, but much of your competition will be charging $300 to $500 per day.

At those prices, $200 a day plus transportation looks like a real bargain to the employer in need of training.

Offering instruction at your home or office to one person at a time is not likely to reap the profits your other options will. For one thing, the travel time makes it less convenient for your customers, so they're not willing to pay as much.

For another, it demands that you set aside a room dedicated to training and equip it with all the standard classroom furnishings: desk, blackboard, and one very nice computer system. This requires a somewhat larger initial investment and more maintenance. Let's face it, word of mouth won't work for you if your machine's down half the time and the training room looks like the bear pit at the San Diego Zoo. On the other hand, if you hate to leave home . . .

If you want to train at home, and if you've got the money for four or five systems, setting up a complete classroom is not a bad idea at all. Do check with your state and local authorities first. We know one place that launched a training center only to have it shut down, for lack of state certification, hours after their first ad appeared—and weeks after the systems had been paid for.

In the southern Connecticut area, students pay a flat fee up front for the entire course; tuition seems to be pegged at $10 to $15 per hour. Clearly, if you can entice four or five people to enroll in every course you offer, you can get rolling pretty quickly. In fact, at $10 per student hour, thirty-six student hours a week (three three-hour classes, each with four students) will pay off the purchase price and first-year service contract on five computers inside of a year. . . .

How to Train

Earlier we talked about patience; here we stress it again. People are paying you good money because they *don't* know what you know. You must expect them to be ignorant.

And they expect you to be professional. Be ready to prepare manuals, plot classroom exercises, and assign homework. You are *not* a friend sitting down saying, "Hey, lemme show you something neat!" For the duration of the course, you are their instructor, and it is, ultimately, your responsibility to ensure that they have every opportunity to learn.

Immediately after you've introduced yourself to your class, remind them to be patient with themselves. They should not expect to pick up the material up quickly unless they have a lot of prior experience with computers and similar software packages. If they do . . . you might suggest, as a friend, that while you appreciate their money, they could probably find better ways of spending it.

Whatever category you're teaching, start at the very beginning and work your way up to the complicated stuff. "This is a computer" is not a bad opening line.

Try to structure your lessons so that, with the exception of your opening line, everything builds on something you have already said. Talking about the cursor before someone has seen it sheds no light on anything.

In other words, you can't just walk in and teach. You must prepare your classes in advance.

You have a computer. Use it now. Load your word-processing package and sketch a course.

Begin at the beginning. What are you teaching? Why do your pupils want to study it? What will they be able to do once they have mastered it?

What is the simplest thing they can do with it? Teach that, first. Give them a sense of accomplishment right at the very outset.

Okay, they've got that—what's next? What's the next simplest thing they can do (preferably using what they've already learned)? Explain it, and let them do it right away.

This hands-on experience is crucial. You must let them *do* what you're teaching them to do. If they're reluctant, push them. Don't let them sit back and just watch and listen. They will not learn.

Be thorough as you advance through the subject matter. Don't schedule digressions into your course outline, but if something you say triggers a question, answer it right away, even if it concerns something you're going to cover in more detail later. Your student has made an association between the two; reinforce the association, don't weaken it.

Besides, the students know why they want to learn what you're teaching. Their questions probably relate to something specific they want to do with it. *Encourage* questions—only they will tell you what your students don't know.

Remember that when you come right down to it, you

are not teaching them, you are helping them to teach themselves.

That is why, once the basics are out of the way, you should find out if they have any unique applications and teach *those*. Expand from there.

It might mean more work for you. It might mean rewriting your course materials for each new class. But do it anyway. You'll find your customers will learn much more quickly if you're teaching them how to do exactly what they want to do. They'll be happier, too.

And they'll be much more likely to join your good-buddy network when the course is done.

CHAPTER 8

You Can Get It for Them Wholesale

Imagine a horn of plenty, brimming with software, supplies, equipment, and peripherals—all free. Imagine never having to buy a box of disks, a package of printer ribbons, or a carton of form-feed paper—ever again! Imagine *earning* money, instead of spending it, every time you open a computer-supply catalogue.

It's not a dream. Thousands of people are doing it, right now, and you can do it too. How?

Buy low and sell just a little higher. It's as simple as that. For example:

Your printer uses Diablo Hytype I multistrike ribbons, and you'd like to buy a box of a dozen. At $4.Ø5 each, you'll pay $48.6Ø. But if you buy eight dozen, you get a bulk discount: at $3.5Ø each, or $42.ØØ per dozen, eight dozen cost $336.ØØ. Now, what if you sold the extra seven dozen ribbons for $4.ØØ each?

Not at all coincidentally, 7 × 12 × 4 = 336. You've just

earned a free box of ribbons—and saved your customers sixty cents per box, too.

That's pleasant—but now let's sweeten the deal a little more. Here's a catalogue from a mail-order supply house, offering the same ribbons at a bulk price of $3.25 each. Now you can get eight dozen for only $312.00! Let's add $5.00 for shipping, for a total cost of $317.00. The result? A free box of ribbons, *and* a $19.00 profit!

Of course, this system only works if you can sell the extra ribbons, which brings us to the first law of computer entrepreneurship: Know Thy Market. Your Diablo Hytype ribbons won't move very fast if everyone around you is using the Wang multistrike cartridge. This is one of the few situations in which it is to your advantage to want what everyone else wants.

Solution? Find out what everyone else wants. A short ad in your local alternative newspaper, offering convenience and promising savings, will attract others who want the same supplies as you do. If you hear from seven people, each of whom wants a dozen ribbons, place an order for eight dozen! Sell the surplus to your new customers at just a little over your cost (to cover shipping and the price of the advertisement). Gain three good things:

1. New friends, delighted with their savings
2. Free ribbons
3. The opportunity to get more good deals for your new friends, and more free stuff for yourself

This works well for items offered at bulk or special sale prices. But what about higher-priced goodies like modems, memory buffers, and printers? Could you possible get them free, too?

Of course! Like this:

You want a Diablo metal printwheel. One printwheel costs $63.00. But if you buy six or more from that discount mail-order house, each one costs only $50.00. Savings on each: $13.00. Let's say you pass along $5.00 of that savings, bringing the price you charge to $58.00. How many printwheels must you sell in order to get a free one for yourself?

$50.00 per printwheel divided by $8.00 per printwheel—your gross profit on each wheel = 6.25 printwheels.

You can't sell one quarter of a printwheel, so make it seven. If you can find just seven people who want what you want—at a discount!—you get your printwheel free.

I hope that by now you are convinced: unless you need something right this minute—and the only time you need it right this minute is when you must complete a job *now*—rushing to your local computer retailer is the wrong way to buy computer equipment, peripherals, and supplies. With just a bit of time and thought, you can pay less for your own things, help other people pay less for their things, and sometimes get things free while earning money.

Now let's look at a few more ways to do that. The first method doesn't require you to buy or sell anything at all!

It's called earning a "finder's fee," and you must arrange it with your supplier in advance. It works like this. You keep your eyes and ears open for sales prospects—people might want to buy computers, peripherals, or supplies. You pass their names along to your supplier. The supplier won't reveal your name unless you say it's okay to do so. If your tip results in a sale, you get a finder's fee, the amount depending on the size of the sale. That's all you do, and by doing it you can earn as much as several hundred dollars.

The second method requires that you actually sell the equipment, but since you already own it yourself, that shouldn't be too difficult. Example: You own a Xerox 820-II, with two eight-inch disk drives, and Diablo printer. Your neighbor is thinking about installing a system in her law office, but she doesn't have time to sit through a dozen sales presentations from different suppliers. You're very happy with the 820-II (or whatever system you own), and you know that similar equipment would meet her needs, too.

So you set up a demonstration and invite her over. You show her the features of your system and how they apply to her needs. You sit her down in front of the terminal and let her see for herself how easy it is to learn. You offer a package: installation, training, and help with computerizing her work.

Meanwhile, you've already made a deal with your supplier. If you make the sale, all the supplier does is ship the merchandise; you do the rest. Many suppliers will offer as much as a 10 percent commission on this arrangement. That can mean as much as $1200—or more—for you.

This deal makes at least three people happy: your neighbor, who gets a good system *and* a trainer/installer in whom she already has confidence; your supplier, who sells another system; and you. You get your commission and the satisfaction of seeing another happy computer owner in your neighborhood.

You can take this a bit farther if you care to make an investment. What if you buy the equipment yourself? You might get as much as 25 percent off the price your supplier would charge someone else. Now you turn around and sell it to your neighbor; again, the package you sell includes installation, training—say, forty hours' worth—and help with application.

Let's say you buy a $12,000 system for $9000 and sell it for $11,000. You get $2000, and your neighbor still makes out like a bandit, saving $1000 and gaining a good, convenient, sympathetic helper. You can call the $2000 a 22 percent return on your investment, if you like—or perhaps you'd rather think of yourself as a fifty-dollar-an-hour computer consultant. Either way, everybody wins.

The moral to all this: Don't buy retail if you can help it. And don't discount your own time, knowledge, and experience. Too many people believe that if they can do a thing, it must not be worth very much. That's not true! Familiarity with your own home computer makes you valuable. After all, you're the one who had the nerve to go out and buy a computer in the first place. You spent the money, and you devoted time to learning how to run the machine. You familarized yourself with peripherals, supplies, and the most economical ways to get them. Don't you deserve a return on your investment?

Of course you do. Here is another way to get that return, while arranging for others to benefit by your experience.

Perhaps one of the reasons you bought a computer was to teach your children computer literacy. Other parents want that for their children, too. But buying a home computer for a child can be a hair-raising experience: How to choose among the many brands and models offered? How to decide which computer offers the most educational value? How to figure out which one the little monste— . . . uh, darling, will actually *use?*

You can help. And you can make money doing it. If you know the equipment well enough to offer installation, training, and further support, you can buy the equipment by mail and sell it to parents who want educational computers for their children. Or you can make one of the arrangements described above with your manufacturer or distributor. You've got the knowledge and the customers; they've got the equipment. Surely you can come to an understanding that benefits everyone—including yourself, of course.

One word of warning in all this: whatever you're selling, or reselling, make sure you know exactly what the warranty and service arrangements are, and state these clearly to your customers. Sooner or later someone is going to have to repair the computer. Local service is a necessity, and a service contract is more than a frill, especially when the system is heavily used. Keep copies of any warranties or service contracts entered into by your customers; your knowledge and the proper documentation will simplify matters immensely when the gadget develops a glitch.

In fact, it's your knowledge that makes it all possible, from your first "free" box of disks to the $2500 fee you may earn as a computer-buying consultant to the local law firm. Those savings and profits derive directly from knowledge you have acquired in learning to use your own home computer. A retail computer store offers that knowledge for sale, in the form of installation, training, and further support. The cost of this knowledge is included in the retail price of what they sell. If you've already got it, why buy it again? Why not, in fact, sell it—just the way they do?

Conversely, the less knowledge you have, the more you should acquire—for a price, if necessary. Don't try to sell or use knowledge that you don't yet have. If you need help learning to use a buffer, for example, and can't yet compare intelligently among the various brands and models of them, don't try to buy one from a mail-order house and resell it.

The old writer's rule, Write What You Know, goes for writing sales orders, too.

A couple of tips bear mentioning here. When buying computers, peripherals, and supplies from a mail-order house, whether for yourself or for resale, take the same precautions as you would when buying anything else. Check with the Better Business Bureau. Get the details of any warranties, and get the name of the salesperson with whom you're dealing. Pay by personal check when you can; if you run into trouble with the company, you can stop the check. It's harder to recall a credit-card charge, and if they've got a money order (as good as cash) you may be out of luck. Finally, *know what you want.* A mail-order house is not a good place to shop by phone.

You, of course, will want to act fairly and honorably, too. As long as you are honest and up-front about any arrangements you make, you will have little difficulty while your business is small. Should you begin selling regularly by mail, you might want to affiliate yourself with the Direct Mail Marketing Association, the professional organization of the direct-mail industry. Call your local Better Business Bureau for the address.

And while we're on the subject of honesty—don't sell copied software. That is, don't make and sell duplicates of copyrighted programs. To do so is a criminal offense. You want your knowledge and talent to generate profits and satisfaction, not jail terms and $5ØØØ fines.

You'll notice that throughout this discussion we've stressed the good things everyone can get from your use of your computer knowledge. This is a little-discussed but very important side effect that occurs whenever people exercise real intelligence: things get better for everyone around them, too. If you know how to buy good-quality diskettes cheaply, you *and* your associates derive the benefit. If you know how to identify potential computer buyers, your local distributor will be as happy to hear about them as you are to accept a finder's fee.

Let me point out here that you will be prudent *not* to set yourself up in *competition* with your local computer businesses, nor in any way to make adversaries of them. Sending your friends to the local retail outlet to "try out" the computers, then reeling them back to yourself and your trusty mail-order catalogue, is a sure way to make enemies. Pushing equipment or supplies that you know are unsuited to a customer's needs will sour people on computers in general, and make you look lower than the Mariana Trench in the eyes of others in the computer business. Visibly snatching customers from beneath the noses of other vendors is not recommended, either. In fact, it's a good idea to *send* them customers when you find people whose needs—for knowledge or for equipment—you cannot satisfy.

In short, the safest and most comfortable place for a small-time computer-wheeler-and-dealer to be is in a civil if not cordial relationship with other local computer businesses. They can hurt you a lot more than you can hurt them, and they can probably help you more than you can help them, too. You don't want to compete with them.

Unless, of course, you do want to compete with them. Maybe you've discovered you like the business of selling computers. Maybe you think you're pretty good at it, and you want to do more. What then?

Well, you can go to work for someone else. Or you can go into business for yourself. Let's look at the first option.

Selling computers is just like selling cars, except that cars are dumb and you can't drive a computer—yet. To succeed in selling computers for a retailer or manufacturer, you will need the very same equipment as the successful car salesperson. Except in the area of product knowledge, your sales kits will contain these same items:

1. A good sales personality. This is one of the most important attributes of the successful salesperson. Are you the shy and retiring type, reluctant to assert yourself and your ability? If so, you'll have to change before you'll succeed in sales. And even if you are the original hail-fellow-well-met, you'll also need

2. A real liking for the job. Selling is hard work. You'd better like it, because if you plan to make a career of it you're going to be doing it a lot.

3. Desire is a big requirement, too. Your desire to succeed must transcend fatigue, discouragement, rejection, setbacks, and uncertainty. And in the face of all these things, you must retain as well your

4. Belief that you will succeed. Most salespeople work at least partly on commission. In general, people who choose to take small salaries get bigger percentage commissions on their sales, and vice versa. This is just one example of the way your belief in yourself will put you in line for success—but you must believe *first.*

If you possess all these requirements, start by selling yourself—to the presidents of the companies you want to work for. Find out all about them, and choose the companies that offer the best opportunities and rewards. Write a letter convincing them that you're a genuine diamond of a salesperson, even if you're not an experienced one. Many companies want to do the polishing themselves, in training programs tailored to their special requirements.

Finally, when you go to the interview, remember that first impressions count—maybe more than anything else. Your interviewer will try to imagine how you would represent his computer company. Therefore, present yourself accordingly. You are already demonstrating your sales technique—with yourself as the product.

The potential rewards and possibilities for advancement in computer sales are enormous. A six-figure annual income is not uncommon. It is possible also to gain promotion into specialized sales-support areas—custom programming and systems design for industrial users, for example. The sky really is the limit here.

To reach it, though, you will work very hard. Be ready for sixty- to eighty-hour weeks, at least at first, and be ready for plenty of challenge and stress. Besides the business of computers, you'll need to learn the businesses of your customers in considerable detail. You'll need to become adept at translating the features of your product into advantages for the potential buyer. You'll have to deal, efficiently and assertively, with not one but two business organizations at the same time: your customer's, and your own.

It's not all glamorous travel and long lunches with clients —not by a long shot. The amount of paperwork needed to process and complete a sale prompted one highly successful computer salesperson to remark that the job really begins *after* the deal is made.

When asked the drawbacks of a career in sales, the

same executive replied only half-jokingly, "I don't expect to live past sixty! But—it's worth it. The challenge, the satisfaction of making the sale and keeping the customer happy, the exhilaration of knowing I'm being rewarded for my own ability and drive—it's absolutely worth it!"

If things can be good in a computer-sales career, can they be better if you're in business for yourself?

The answer: a resounding *maybe*—with plenty of reservations. The climate for starting a computer store or business of your own is intensely competitive. You'll need all the drive, perseverence, and skill of the company-employed salesperson—and more. You'll need the commitment to invest sixteen hours a day, six or seven days a week, for at least two years, probably longer. You'll need good health, good luck, and the sympathetic understanding of your friends and family.

But beyond all this, there is another requirement for starting your own computer business, one that you must have on top of all the others. More than time and drive and knowledge and perseverence, you need *capital.*

Money. Starting a business—your own or a franchise—takes lots and lots. And now that computer stores have sprung up everywhere, it's harder to get the needed capital from the bank. Says one independent computer entrepreneur, "These guys are dropping out like flies in the face of the cutthroat competition, and the banks are taking it in the neck. A few years ago, they'd jump to lend you the start-up money—but not anymore. They're cautious—they have to be. It's their job. They want to see how you do on your own *before* they risk lending money to you."

Just how much money is involved?

"I don't think it can be done for less than a hundred thousand," says the same entrepreneur. "Consider that it costs twenty-five thousand just to set up a training and conference room. You can't really sell if you don't offer support, and you can't give the support without somewhere to give it. Chairs, tables, carpet—it's very expensive." He continues:

"It's not only that it costs money to set up properly—you need money before you can make a deal. In effect, you have to own the equipment before you can sell it. You can't very well ask your customer for the money in advance. So the amount of capital you control limits the amount of business you can do, the size of the account you can handle. There are many accounts I could sell, if I had the capital to do it. Furthermore, the size of your capital determines the number of setbacks you can absorb without going under. If I were to give advice to someone considering starting out right now, I'd say one word: Don't."

Which is not to say that it *can't* be done—only that it's difficult. We're talking hardball here, and the pitchers are throwing fast—right at your head. Let's say you start a computer store on Main Street, and offer several systems: IBM, Xerox, Timex/Sinclair, and Osborne, for example.

Remember that beyond the costs of operating the store—rent, phone, utilities, salaries, supplies, furnishings, and the rest—you have shouldered a financial commitment to each of those companies. You are obliged to take a certain number—say, four units—from each manufacturer, every month. This is the agreement under which the manufacturers supply you with the product you sell. Perhaps you get some of your products from distributors, who may not require you to take any minimum number of units, but who charge you more for each one. That gives you a slimmer profit margin, because people won't buy the machines if you charge too much for them.

And you must sell the machines, because you have to pay your suppliers for the batch you're going to take next month. That's right—you pay your suppliers in advance, but you get paid after you make the sale. And that, in a nutshell, is why you need so much capital. You can't just hang in thin air until someone comes in to buy a word processor. You've got to have money available to keep things going in the meantime.

Nevertheless, after a time you do establish a comfortable profit margin, largely because you're the only computer store in town. You sell good equipment, and you give good service and training, too. Next year you might even start to make a little money for yourself. (You didn't expect to be taking home any money the first year, did you?)

At any rate, everyone's happy until the new kid moves in, right down the street. Turns out he wants to own a computer business, too. The trouble is, you started with a hundred thousand bucks, but he's got two hundred thousand. That means, among other things, that he can spend a hundred thousand making his store more attractive, cutting his profit margin, stocking more kinds of equipment, offering price breaks, giving more free service and training.

He's putting you out of business. The manufacturers are just as happy to supply him as they are to supply you. The customers like him better, naturally, because he's offering them a lot more for their money. Your territory is in no way protected. There is absolutely no one to stop him—except you.

You, with your third mortgage, your kids in school, your grocery bills, and your wheezing Chevrolet, in which you make sales calls from early morning until late at night.

You, with your damned dream, which still might, just *might* make you rich, if you find a way to win what's turning into a no-holds-barred price war.

That's how it will work.

Still interested?

You can make it work. You can, that is, if you're smart and careful and in excellent health; if you really know your computers and your customers, and know how to run a business; and if you're well capitalized and very, very lucky.

And if you stop selling machinery, and start selling solutions to customers' problems.

That's the key. It all comes back to the knowledge in your head. From the first bulk-discounted box of floppy disks to the last quarter-million-dollar system that you sell, the key to success in computer sales is not selling machines. It's finding problems and solving them well.

The first sales problem you may face is "My buddies and I need disks. How can we get them cheaply, and still get quality?" That problem, in its essence, is not much different from "I've got a million-dollar computer-driven robot assembly system, and it doesn't do exactly what I want it to do. Can you help me?"

To solve the second problem, you need more knowledge and more capital than you need to solve the first. What you don't need is a cute little corner computer store, complete with staggering overhead expenses. True, a home office doesn't have the quaint, romantic appeal of your own store—but then neither does bankruptcy court.

To sum up: You deserve a return on the investment you made in your home computer. You may choose to get that return in a small way, by shopping intelligently for your own needs and the needs of your acquaintances, or you may want to put in more time and thought, and get bigger rewards. You may decide to take risks and increase your potential return on investment even more. You will not, of course, decide to take silly risks, based on dreams rather than fact. You know there's nothing dreamlike about the computer business.

But exercised well, your investment and your knowledge will make life better for you and everyone around you.

That, friends, is capitalism at work. You're already part of it. The home computer is one of the most marvelously efficient "capitalist tools" ever invented. It will enable you to make and save money. All you have to do is use it.

So use it. Don't just sit there at the terminal.

Learn—and earn!

CHAPTER 9

Can a Piece of Your Mind Offer Them Peace of Mind?

Within five years, almost every American will own a microcomputer. The development and dispersal of the home computer is repeating the pattern of pocket calculators: introduced in small quantities and at exorbitant prices, their production and their sales skyrocketed as prices plunged to 2Ø percent, 1Ø percent, and finally 2 percent of what they were at the outset. The same thing is happening in computers.

Another part of the calculator pattern will also repeat: before too long, a lot of people will have grown impatient with the limitations of the machines they learned on, and will be on their second, third, or even fourth systems.

And unlike unwanted, outgrown calculators, which fit neatly in a desk drawer "just in case," home computers tend to be on the bulky side. Especially in their packing crates, they are inconveniently sized to be kept around for a rainy day. People will sell them at painful losses, or let them collect dust, steal storage space, and grow ever more irritating with their reminder of money down the drain.

The waste will leave a bitter taste in owners' mouths, an emptiness in their wallets, and a fervent wish in their hearts that they had bought the right machine the first time out.

Preventing that bitterness presents you with yet another possibility for your VSB: computer consulting.

What would you be if you became a computer consultant? You'd be a troubleshooter, an investment counselor, a problem solver, a trainer, a coordinator, a programmer, a recommender, an administrator—any or all of the preceding, as you choose.

That's the nice part: you choose. Figure out which of those elements you enjoy and are good at (see chapter 3 if you need some help), then configure your VSB so that's what you do. Just make sure potential customers understand from the very beginning the limits to the service you provide.

Whether you go directly into it, or guide the evolution of a service VSB toward it, you'll find it challenging, rewarding, and very enjoyable. Not to mention profitable.

The way we see it, you can offer consultation at five different, increasingly responsible levels. At your option, you can confine your VSB to one level only, or offer all five and let the customers choose the service they're most comfortable with.

The In-Laws' Dream

If you've ever wanted to get paid for giving advice, this is what you've been looking for. At this, the simplest consultation level, you offer your clients an analysis of their needs, and a recommendation as to which system or systems would best fill those needs. You bill them for the time you spent studying their operations and writing up your recommendations.

A delightful variant on this theme involves clients who have already analyzed their needs, and hire you merely as an evaluator. All they want is for you to tell them which systems answer their needs.

The Purchasing Agent

Here you go a bit further: after analyzing your customers' requirements, you purchase (with their authorization) the systems that best satisfy those requirements. If you have contacts with a fair number of suppliers, this could be very advantageous to both you and your clients—your contacts should give you a discount off retail, some or all of which you can pass along. You bill for your time. If possible, you take a small commission on the sale of the equipment.

The Hardware Store

A mere step down the road from the purchasing agent lies the hardware store. At this level you offer, of course, an analysis of your customers' needs; you purchase for them the systems that best do what they need to have done; and then you personally supervise the delivery and the physical installation of their equipment. When crates of equipment roll into an office, noncomputer types derive much assurance from the physical presence of the person responsible for their having spent so much money. Being there, plugging the system in, and running whatever diagnostics package comes with it allows you to charge extra. Silly, but true.

The Perfectionist

At this level, you guarantee your clients that you will not only deliver their systems, and make certain that they work, but also that *they* know how to make them work. You train them. Perhaps not personally—after reading chapter 7 you might have decided that training is not your forte—but you can certainly locate and hire a free-lance trainer for the day or two it will take to familiarize your customers with the equipment. Naturally you fold the trainer's price (plus a few bucks for the cost of finding the trainer) into whatever you charge.

The Compleat Packager

The ultimate in computer consulting is to provide a total turn-key service: needs analysis, hardware purchase and installation, staff training, and any requisite special programming. Again, you don't have to do the training and programming yourself. It is legal (and desirable, even) to hire specialists for those tasks. What you are selling is *not* your expertise as a CP/M trainer and COBOL programmer; you are selling the ability to satisfy the customers' needs. And believe us, you bill accordingly.

Sounds Great, but—

—how do you do it?

It's not easy, but neither is it *that* hard. Thousands of people across the country are already doing it, and many of them aren't doing it impartially. Those folks are working for—and getting paid by—the companies whose systems they will ultimately recommend.

Before You Start

Your first step is to become utterly objective. Sure you have an Apple IIe which you love about yea much less than life, sexual liberty, and money in the bank. If, however, all you recommend to your accounts are Apple IIe's, you will lose credibility—and clients—in very short order. Not because there's anything wrong with the IIe, but simply because it is not the *best* machine for *all* applications.

A funny thing about computer owners is that they tend to recommend, almost exclusively, the systems they own. It has a little to do with familiarity, and a lot to do with pride. Who among us cares to admit an expensive mistake? Rather than that, most of us would rather tout the superiority of the systems in which we invested our own hard-earned dollars.

This attitude will sink your VSB quicker than a torpedo will a rowboat.

You *must* become familiar with every system available for sale in your area. We're not talking the sixty-five-dollar membrane keyboard systems, here. We're talking office-quality systems; computers that can stand up to eight hours of use a day, five days a week, with service calls few and far between. We're talking microcomputers that will *satisfy your clients' needs*—and let's face it, you're not going to get much business from people whose only desire is to play *Donkey Kong* for free.

How do you develop this sort of familiarity? In three ways. First, you scan your local newspapers daily for announcements of free "seminars"—usually half- or full-day sales pitches thrown by retailers, distributors, or manufacturers. Not only does this further justify the tax deduction you take for your newspaper subscription (see chapter 12), it lets you see a lot of systems, and meet a lot of sales reps.

Second, you meet the sales reps. This is important. While manufacturers will usually be reluctant to grant a consultant any sort of discount, distributors and retailers are an entirely different story. These people *have to move their hardware*. If they don't, their inventory swells and their bank charges zoom. You'll find that many, if not all, are amenable to selling at a little over cost if all they have to do is process your order and ship to the designated address. (Review also the section on mail order in chapter 2.)

Third, and even more important, you see the systems. As a consultant, what you're selling is your ability to single out the one computer that will best meet your customers' needs. The only way you will develop that ability is by collecting literature (and damn near memorizing it), attending demonstrations, asking questions, and actually experimenting with the hard- and software yourself.

Do, by the way, identify yourself as a consultant. First and foremost, it's the ethical thing to do. Second, if you conduct yourself properly, you'll find that distributors and retail store managers will work with someone who might move twenty or thirty systems for them year in and year out. . . .

On the Job

Chapter 3 talked about how you determine the skills you're going to use in your VSB. Pull out that list you made back then, because to succeed as a consultant you *must* (1) know how to ask questions, and (2) know how to *listen* to answers.

Remember, the object of consulting is not merely to computerize your client's office in the most efficient, economical way possible—it's to do all that and please your customer at the same time.

Hand in Hand We Go

The process is a joint venture from word one. You must involve your customers at every stage; you must take their feedback into account. Customers who do not contribute to the final selection and implementation will, in the long run, be unhappy. You can not impose solutions on your clients.

So the first thing you do is sit down and talk. Be prepared to spend *as much time as is needed* coming to a complete understanding of each account's objectives, criteria, applications, and budget. Ask the questions straight out: "Why do you want a computer? What do you think it will do for you? What particular tasks do you have for it?"

Their *objectives* will tend to be a little fuzzy around the edges, and be expressed as goals for the future: higher profits, increased efficiency, 15 percent faster turn-around time, 20 percent lower overtime costs.

You have to be ready to tell your customers whether their objectives are realistic or fanciful. A lot of people have exaggerated notions about a microcomputer's capabilities. You *must* disillusion them. You may lose their business by telling them the truth, but better that than a lawsuit later.

In contrast, *criteria* are more like standards for the present. They may include specifics like a green CRT screen, a 160 cps printer, or vendors of a certain quality. Defining these hard-and-fast standards in the beginning will save you many headaches later on.

Applications, meanwhile, are the specific tasks the clients want done on their computers: typing 300-page documents through four revision cycles; billing 623 clients quarterly; paying 47 employees weekly. You must question the clients closely until you have determined the scope and complexity of each task. You must also establish each task's relative importance in that office: What percent of a working day does it consume? What has to get done first? Where is eight-decimal-place accuracy crucial?

The last essential part of these exploratory sessions is discovering your customers' *budgets:* How much money are they willing to spend? A law office, for example, might want a computer for wills, evictions, and other boiler-plate documents. That's a perfectly rational application—but if they think they can do it for $15ØØ, they're lost in cloud-cuckoo-land, and you have to say so. Tactfully, of course. . . .

Once you have defined a customer's objectives, criteria, applications, and budget, write them down. Make certain that your customer agrees with them. Give a copy to your client and keep a copy for yourself. This will serve as the initial outline for your automation strategy.

Look for Point of Impact

Now it's time to study your customer's current procedures. Having determined what the office is supposed to be doing, you talk to the actual workers to find out precisely how they are doing it.

Look for bottlenecks. Where is work backing up? Why is it backing up there? In some accounts, the problem will lie in the file cabinets—manual retrieval of paper-based records could be taking too much time. In other accounts, the workflow will slow to a trickle at the stage where forms are filled in using the data from those file cabinets. Still other offices will snarl up at the typists' desks, as rough drafts and revisions fill in-baskets faster than final copies do out-baskets.

You are the hot-shot consultant. You have to find those bottlenecks. Granted, your client might already have pointed all of them out for you—but don't count on it. Ask questions, listen to the answers, and then check for yourself.

At the same time, you should probe for problems no one tells you about. This office has been living with its situation for some time; the staff just might have learned to live with less-than-ideal conditions. Your recommendations could move things along much more quickly—if you can find the invisible problems.

So don't be afraid to ask if they meet all their deadlines, or have to pay people overtime, or need to bring in temporary help now and then. Forget shyness. Be brazenly curious. Remember, they are paying you to ask the right questions. So ask, already.

Select the Tools

Once you've identified the problem areas, the bottlenecks in the workflow, it's time to figure out how to unclog them. This always involves a combination of software and hardware: the specific off-the-shelf program that will best handle their unique application, and the hardware that will run that software most quickly and reliably.

As we've said elsewhere in this book, pick the software first. When you're advising someone to buy a system to handle a finite number of discrete applications, the software is much more important than the hardware.

Fortunately, the really good software is in such great demand that the manufacturers have brought out versions for most standard hardware configurations.

What software will do the job best? Frankly, if you don't have the experience to find candidate packages and evaluate them, you shouldn't be attempting to get into this business.

But Where Does It All Go?

Once you've determined which applications package or packages will handle the job(s)—and *before* you settle on the hardware—take a good, hard look at how much room the office has for its system(s). Here on this page the notion of a "space analysis" sounds absurd, but very few offices waste space. Even the most compact system will probably require more room than the typewriter it's replacing.

If things look at all tight, buy some graph paper (although it's flashier if you can do the whole thing on your own machine). Draw a floor plan, inking in all permanent fixtures. Use cutouts scaled to the appropriate size to represent all the furniture that has to go into that office. Cutouts of a different color can stand for the computer(s). Now move everything around on your floor plan till you've proven conclusively that it all fits.

Be very careful about environmental concerns here. Printers are *noisy.* If the room is so small that the printer has to sit right next to someone's ear, someone is going to be miserable unless that printer runs but once in a blue moon. Many disk drives have fans, and the steady whir will drive other people straight up the walls. A light shining on a CRT screen at the wrong angle will create intolerable glare, and send somebody home with a headache day in and day out.

Sometimes you'll discover that for a system to fit into a room, the office may need either new furniture or custom carpentry. This is not necessarily a bad thing for you. On the one hand, many of your electronics suppliers also carry lines of computer furnishings and are willing to offer the same discount off list; on the other, it never hurts to make friends with carpenters. What *is* a bad thing is not foreseeing the need.

What's worse is recommending something even though you know it won't fit, or will drive the staff crazy if you can cram it in.

Remember, your goal is to make everyone happy. If the machine destroys office morale because people trip over it, or it's too noisy, or it blinds them, that machine will *lower* productivity. Your clients will not be getting their money's worth.

So be honest. If they can't do it, they can't do it. It's your duty to say so.

The Cost Analysis

You've done all the research. It's time to make your recommendation. Do you just list the prices for hardware, software, and supplies and think you have, thereby, summed up the cost of the system?

Of course not. There is a big difference between the cost of buying and the cost of *owning.* Many buyers are aware of that, and will ask you to provide a comprehensive idea of what it will cost in time as well as in money. One system may retail for more than another, yet be a better bargain in the long run. Your clients won't know which is which until you tell them.

How long does the system take to learn? How quickly will it do the job it's being bought for? How often does it break down? How good are the available service agreements? Can repairs be made quickly, on site?

You really ought to include these considerations when you tell your clients what their computers will cost. It's possible that they'd rather believe the former used-car salesman at the corner computer store who says his machine never crashes—but if you *don't* warn them about these "expenses," you're the one who'll be blamed when they crop up.

Here's where you reaffirm their commitment to the budget they cited you at the outset. If they start shaking their heads and "tsk-tsking" at the price, it's also time for a reassessment of their objectives.

The Benefits Analysis

Sometimes your customers will ask you to deliver this in conjunction with the cost analysis. Its purpose is to justify the investment of time and money you're asking them to make by outlining the sorts of returns those investments will yield.

A word of caution: be careful about putting actual numbers on paper. If you predict annual benefits of $7,350, and a year from now they can only find $3000 worth, you could have problems. Especially if they kept that piece of paper. . . .

What generally works well is to show how your recommendation achieves the objectives they laid down at the exploratory sessions, how it meets their criteria, and how it handles their applications, all while staying in budget.

Insofar as is possible, document time saved on a per-job basis. Many businesses are reluctant to share payroll costs with an outsider, and will want to calculate the annual savings for themselves. Converting time saved to dollars is a task they may want to handle on their own. From your point of view, this is just dandy. Numbers they derive by themselves will carry more weight than numbers you provide.

Repeat this for any savings realized by doing for themselves jobs they used to send out—like typesetting press releases, or maintaining a small mailing list.

Further, if the system adds any intangible value to

whatever they produce there—by heightening accuracy, enhancing typescript appearance, shortening response times—you mention these prominently. Here you won't have to worry about the time value of a better-looking typed page. Just make sure they know it's part of the return they'll get.

For your own information, and on a separate sheet of paper, work all the numbers out and add up the value of all the benefits. Subtract from that the total costs. That's the "profit" on their investment, if you will.

Take a good hard look at that number. If your clients could get a better return on their money by stashing the cash in a bank, either they shouldn't buy a computer, or you've done your numbers wrong. Double-check.

Most of the time, though, that number should represent anything from a 2Ø percent to a 5Ø percent return on investment. Some customers will specifically ask to see it, in which case you oblige. If they don't ask, don't force it on them, but do make certain that they understand its general order of magnitude.

No Surprise Parties, Please!

Once you have everything selected—the software, the hardware, the workstation's location—and once the decision-maker has reviewed your recommendations and agreed with them, you should set up an "implementation calendar." Although this is more important for large offices buying several systems, even small offices will find it worthwhile.

In essence, an implementation calendar is a timetable that specifies as precisely as possible when everything will happen. It includes the dates on which all equipment arrives, when installation occurs, when training takes place, when primary applications are first performed, when bills must be paid . . . the works.

You do it because the very last thing you want is to disrupt totally the office routine, and some disruption will be inevitable. You must minimize the uproar. It's part of what you're getting paid for.

Clearly, this will require close coordination with all your suppliers. The first few times out, you're pretty much at their mercies—but if you find that they consistently louse up your schedules, look for new vendors.

Even more important is making certain that your customers agree with your calendar. Again, don't impose it on them. Sit down and discuss it. Listen to them. If they say it looks too quick, stretch it out—they might have a cash flow problem that would embarrass them if the bills hit too close together. If they say it's too slow, speed things up. One more time: Your goal is to keep your clients happy, because a happy client joins the good-buddy network and generates business for you. An angry customer costs you money.

Finally, make sure everything happens as planned. Deliver on every single one of your promises. It might take more effort than you'd figured. It might even cut your profits. In the long run, though, it'll help you make out like a bandit.

But Who's Going to Pay for All That?

Basically, your market consists of two sorts of people: the fearful and the busy.

Fearful? Yes. A lot of people want computers, but are afraid of

Prejudice

Computer-shoppers know they can go either to a retailer selling only one brand, or to an outlet carrying many different makes. At the first kind of store, many buyers can feel that even if the single line carried has no model right for their needs, the sales rep won't admit it. Does an oil sheik endorse solar heating?

The second kind of store fosters wariness of another variety of prejudice. As in any volume business, it has "sleepers"—systems that have not been selling well, that are clogging up the storeroom. There are also top-of-the-line machines, whose higher prices mean higher commissions. Although not every sales rep in every store would ignore customers' needs and deliberately steer them toward the slowest mover or the costliest system, the possibility does exist. The would-be buyer knows this, and can be intimidated right out of the market.

A second fear:

The Wrong Hardware

The cost of software can mount up, but the single most expensive item is the computer itself.

An embarrassment of riches surrounds the buyer, and with it comes indecision. So many lines to choose from; so many models within each line. *What if he picks the wrong one?* If he explains his current needs properly, he might get the right machine, but what if his needs change? Is the system expandable? Can he trade up? *Can he ask the right questions to guarantee the sales rep understands the requirements?* What does he do if the machine proves to be unsatisfactory once he has purchased it?

No one likes to make mistakes, especially one as expensive as buying the wrong machine.

And a third primal fear:

The Wrong Software

Someone with the required hardware is still only halfway home. The machine needs software—and there are tens of thousands of programs on the market. One program costs nowhere near as much as a computer, but selecting exactly the right one can be time-consuming even for an expert. How does a novice choose between two word-processing programs? How does one know whether the software will be easy to use, easy to learn? Will everyone at the office find it equally simple? Often software that doesn't work out can be returned or exchanged, but *what can the customer do if he discovers he's bought the wrong programs after the return period is up?*

Just a few of those thoughts can frighten a lot of people out of the market forever. As can

Fear of Abandonment

New-computer buyers win the Showroom Popularity Award hands down. Sales reps flutter around, hanging on their every word, offering to be helpful in any way possible. Which edge of the double-sided quad density disk goes in first? They'll demonstrate patiently, even if it is for the fifteenth time. What's time when you're spending it with someone you love?

Ah, but once that drive is on the office desk and the buyers simply cannot remember which edge goes in first . . .

But never mind—they'll just make a quick call to those helpful sales reps who'll be ecstatic to take care of it.

Won't they?

Funny, but the reps have all been replaced by a corps of surly strangers who refer callers to the service division, which in turn is out to lunch.

People who fear that they won't get the basic handholding after the sale avoid computer stores.

You must remember those fears when you're looking for customers. They won't necessarily help you *find* potential clients, but they might help you *recognize* them when you meet them. And being able to allay those fears will be the major portion of your sales pitch.

Three other important characteristics of your market:

They're aware, in a vague way, that a computer might help their business.

They can afford to buy one.

And finally, they're a bit too busy to learn the subject well enough to do all the necessary investigations themselves.

To single profitable accounts out of the crowd will be difficult—you'll probably have a lot more luck if they identify themselves to you. Go for the ad in the Yellow Pages, and maybe a small display ad on the financial page of your local Sunday paper.

Mass mailings and telephone solicitation could also work for you, if you concentrate on professional types (doctors, lawyers, etc.) and small businesses. Word of mouth will be a very big help to you. As will

Your Existing Client Base

Should you already have a VSB that offers computer services to uncomputerized businesses, you can ease into consulting from that.

If you've run your other VSB well, your customers don't know how they ever got along without the convenience it provides. You've hooked them on the fruits of the technology.

Better yet, you can tell, just by looking at how much

they pay you every year, whether or not they would save money in the long run by buying their own systems.

If they would, we can bet that it won't be long before they realize that, too.

So why wait till an account wakes up and replaces you with a computer? As soon as you can see a reasonable payback period for them, go tell them the good news.

And you know, it's not a bad idea to warn them at the start of your relationship that this might happen. They might not believe that you'll ever tell them they don't need you anymore, but the thought will linger in their minds. If they do start thinking about a purchase, they'll talk to you first.

And once they talk to you, you have a number of strong selling points in addition to the services everybody offers.

No Snow

They've been dealing with you for a while; they have a fair indication of your reliability. If you've been giving them quality service all along, they know that they can trust you. Most people would much rather deal with a known quantity than with a smooth-talking stranger.

Test Drives

Since you're already performing your clients' applications, you can let them watch the hardware and software in action—or even invite them to sit down and try it out themselves. Other consultants and sales reps can offer demonstrations, but you already have their specific task on disk. Presumably you've developed a letter-perfect way of handling it. Including your methods in the overall package gives you a super edge.

Accurate Maps

Anybody can say, "Doing this, that, and the other will achieve these exact benefits." Not everybody can say that believably.

You can, because you have been doing it for them. This makes your entire benefits analysis that much more trustworthy—and your clients will know that in advance.

Pricing Yourself

What are you worth? Computer consultants are paid on a variety of bases—hourly, daily, per job—but few work for less than twenty-five dollars an hour. If you want to attract business, offer the customer a bargain, but don't underrate yourself, either. Which brings us full circle to, *How much?*

Let's work backward. First you figure out how many hours a year you'd like to devote to your VSB.

Chapter 6 sketches a way for you to decide how much your computer costs you every year. Granted that it won't be running while you're off consulting, you still have to make sure it pays for itself.

Divide computer cost per year by hours per year and you've got computer cost per hour. That's the first component of your hourly charge.

Now you figure your annual overhead—rent, electricity, telephone and Yellow Pages ad, etc.—and derive an overhead cost per hour. That's the second component of your hourly charge.

Finally you estimate what *you* cost per hour. Will five dollars an hour get you away from the TV set? Ten dollars? What is your time worth *to you?*

Add that third component to the first two, and you've got your minimum charge per hour. Tack on extra in cases where the job causes severe inconvenience. If you bill by the job rather than by the hour, you'll learn (through *sigh* trial and error) how long jobs take. In the beginning, you'll probably undercharge consistently.

But that's okay.

When you are first starting out it helps a lot if you price yourself *below* what others are charging for the same service. You don't have their reputations or their experience. You need that competitive edge.

Be careful, though, not to price yourself too low. Your clients might start to doubt your competence. And really, you don't want them to worry about that. After all, you promised to deliver peace of mind, didn't you?

CHAPTER 10

Big Bucks in a Tool Kit

Ah, the lyric loveliness of those three little words, "I'll fix it."

Forget centerfolds. In the Electronic Age, true human beauty resides in the ability to fix a broken computer. We don't care if the the service technician is eight feet tall, has a complexion the color and consistency of library paste, and is carrying one of his heads under his arm. If he has the repair kit under the other arm and knows how to use it, he's okay with us.

You'll feel that way too, when your computer breaks down—which it will, sooner or later. Let's face it; the laws of the universe apply to computers here on earth. One of those laws, simply stated, is this: Things Break. The corollary to this law is simple, also: Things Break Again.

You can turn those laws to your advantage. The proliferation of computers has brought a whole new industry into existence, and it is crying out for qualified workers. People need people who can fix computers. If you are looking for a new job, a new career, or only for a service you can provide from your home in your spare time, computer repair might be for you.

"But," you may be saying, "it's awfully hard to fix computers. I can't possibly understand what goes on inside those things."

Give yourself a little more credit. Didn't you clean the heads on your tape deck last week? Replace the washer in the bathroom faucet? Put a new light switch in the hall? Maybe you even tuned your own automobile.

Computer repair technicians are regular people just like you. It isn't difficult to repair computers; learning how is no insurmountable task, either. And the rewards can be anything from respectable to remarkable.

Consider this: starting salaries at computer repair firms run in the $13,000 to $15,000 range, up to $19,000 or so for a person with an associate's degree in engineering. Those are *starting* salaries. Technicians who work for bigger companies or do more complicated repairs can earn much more, and you can be sure they don't lie awake nights worrying about getting laid off from their jobs. In 1982, sales of a single model of home computer, the Apple II Plus, totaled 15,000 per month. Even if only half those machines need servicing one time each, that's 90,000 repair jobs, or enough work to employ 125 people full time for a year.

You can get in on it. You don't have to be a genius to get steady work and good pay in the field of computer repairs. How?

Let's start with what you don't need.

You don't need legs. The field of electronics is open to the physically disabled person. If you have the use of your hands and enough sight and hearing to do the work, you are a perfect physical specimen for our purposes. Go to it.

You don't need a Ph.D.—or even a bachelor's degree—in anything. You don't need to quit your job, leave home, or invest a lot of money. You don't need to know anything about the insides of computers. You will learn.

What You DO Need—And How to Get It

You need a high school diploma. Any diploma will do. If you don't have one, study up and take the high school equivalency exams in your area. You can buy packaged software to help you prepare for these exams and pass them.

You'll also need a reasonable amount of ability in and knowledge of mathematics. Cast off your math anxiety! We're not talking unified field theory, here. To learn electronics, you have to be able to do algebra and trigonometry. There are computer programs to help you learn them, too.

While you are getting the high school diploma and brushing up your mathematics, investigate the sources of hands-on training in your area. First, check with your local community colleges and vocational schools. Find out what they offer, what it costs, what the programs demand from you, and how much financial aid you may be able to get. Here are the addresses of four computer repair training programs:

Control Data Institute, HQC2AX, 8100 34th Avenue S., Minneapolis, MN 55440
Devry Institute, Bell and Howell, Inc., Dept. 5802, 2201 West Howard Street, Evanston, IL 60202
ITT Institute, 3500 De Pauw Boulevard, PO 68888, Indianapolis, IN 46268
National Education Corporation, Inquiry Dept., 4361 Birch Street, Newport Beach, CA 92663

Find out also what has happened to graduates of the programs you are investigating. Some programs are tailored to prepare people for jobs; others are intended to prepare students for further study. If many of the graduates of a certain program went on to find jobs like the one you want, that program will probably help you, too.

Colleges and vocational schools are not the only institutions that offer training in electronics. There are home-study programs in computer repair. Three of the larger schools for home training in computer repair are:

Cleveland Institute of Electronics, 1776 East 17th Street, Cleveland, OH 44114

NRI Schools, Inc., 3939 Wisconsin Avenue N.W., Washington, DC 20016

National Technical Schools, 4000 South Figueroa Street, Los Angeles, CA 90037

A student in a home-study program must have enough self-discipline and motivation to do the work without the assistance of regular class meetings and assignment deadlines. When questions arise, the student must be aggressive enough to go out and find the answers independently.

Any college, vocational school, or home-study program must be checked out very carefully in advance. Get the answers to the following questions before you enroll or pay any money:

What does the Better Business Bureau say about the program?

How much will it cost to complete the course?

Do you need to buy anything other than books and course material?

How long has the school been established?

With which other educational institutions is it affiliated?

Is it accredited by the National Association of Trade and Technical Schools?

Is it approved by the board of education in your state, or in its home state?

Is it a member of the Association of Independent Schools and Colleges?

Are credits earned in the program transferable to any other educational institutions?

Who are the instructors, and what are their credentials?

What certificate or degree is awarded upon graduation?

How many students who enroll actually manage to complete the program?

How many graduates find jobs in computer repair?

Does the school offer a job placement service to successful graduates? Does the service really work?

What do students and graduates of the program say about it?

What do prospective employers say about the program?

Finally, take a hard look at yourself. If you are considering a "mail-order" education, do you have the discipline and determination to stick with a course of independent study?

There is yet another way to gain a high school diploma and training in electronics, one that will supply all the disciplinary assistance you could ask. Joining the military is not strictly a vocational decision, but the military services do offer education, vocational training, tuition assistance, and other opportunities that may not otherwise be available to you.

If you are interested, investigate carefully what you are getting into *before* you sign on the dotted line. Make sure you know what is guaranteed to you, and what is merely advertised or promised. The armed services are fine and noble organizations with excellent training programs, but their primary purpose is not free education.

Before you enroll in any college, vocational school, or other course of study, talk to repair technicians already working in your area. They can familiarize you with local working conditions, and help you evaluate the educational programs you are considering. You may even capture the interest of a local employer along the way.

Don't expect to learn about particular brands and models of computers during your basic electronics training. You probably won't get that kind of experience until after you have found a job.

Where Are the Jobs?

Where there are computers, there are jobs for people who can fix them. A microcomputer repair technician may work as a field service person, traveling to the customer's location to replace modular components of the computer, or as a bench technician, repairing the malfunctioning components themselves. Generally, employers fall into these categories:

1. **Large computer retailers.** These outlets offer service to their customers, and they train new employees to work on the brands and models of computers they sell. Radio Shack, for example, runs a complete training program consisting of up to eight weeks at a local repair facility, followed by a three-week course on field service and a five-week session on repairing components.

2. **Smaller retail stores.** These may pay less, but may also require fewer formal qualifications from the job applicant. Depending on their size and the arrangements they have made with manufacturers, they may or may not be able to offer brand-specific repair training. Their repair technicians are likely to concentrate on field service, returning defective components to the manufacturer for troubleshooting and repair.

3. **The manufacturers** themselves offer service contracts to their customers and employ repair technicians. Xerox and IBM are two of the largest, offering opportunities to work on a wide range of equipment from home computers to million-dollar business and industrial computer systems.

These companies may require more education and experience from prospective employees; Hewlett-Packard, for example, requires a four-year degree in electrical engineering. In return they offer excellent pay, opportunities for advancement and specialization, and the kinds of benefits only larger companies can afford: pension, insurance, paid vacations, and continuing education, for example. Here are the addresses of some of the major computer manufacturing companies:

Radio Shack, 5ØØ One Tandy Center, Fort Worth, TX 77251

IBM, 1133 Westchester Avenue, White Plains, NY 1Ø6Ø1

Texas Instruments, Data Systems Group, PO 1444, MS 7781, Houston, TX 77251

Burroughs Corporation, Burroughs Place, Detroit, MI 48232

Digital Equipment Corporation, Field Service Group, 146 Main Street, Maynard, MA 48232

Hewlett-Packard, 3000 Hanover Street, Palo Alto, CA 94304

4. Third-party maintenance firms are under contracts with manufacturers to repair computers for their customers. They offer field service and component-level repair for particular brands of equipment like Apple, whose corporate customers are serviced under an exclusive contract with RCA Service Company. Here are the addresses of four third-party maintenance companies:

Western Union Field Service Division, One Lake Street, Upper Saddle River, NJ 07458

TRW, 15 Law Drive, Fairfield, NJ 07006

Sorbus Service, Inc., 50 East Swedesford Road, Frazer, PA 19355

RCA Data Services, Inc., Building 204-2, Route 38, Cherry Hill, NJ 08002

5. Any large organization that uses computers may employ its own service technicians. Users of custom hardware, particularly, need good specialized technical support.

6. Finally, the well-trained and versatile repair technician may work on a **free-lance** basis. Once their warranties have expired, customers may employ anyone they wish to repair their computers. If you're good at it, they will want you. As an independent repair technician, you are likely to be in particularly great demand if there are few repair centers in your locality.

Remember, though, that you will need support from the manufacturers of the equipment you repair; to be efficient, you will need them for technical literature, replacement parts, and help with problems you are not able to resolve.

Service Contracts

As an independent repair technician, you may want to offer service contracts rather than relying on walk-in trade.

A service contract should specify the following:

1. When and where the service is available, and under

what conditions the contract may be extended, changed, or terminated by either party

2. Exactly what service is offered

3. Contingencies and limitations of the contract

4. Payment arrangements

5. What happens if either party is in breach or default of contract

6. What laws govern the execution of the contract

If you plan to offer service contracts, it is a good idea to have your contract checked by a lawyer, to make sure it is legal and correct in your state.

Authorized Service

If you wish to offer "authorized service" for a particular brand, you will need to meet the manufacturer's specialized requirements for becoming authorized. An authorized service arrangement imposes certain obligations on you, both to the company authorizing you and to the customer.

Requirements for becoming an authorized brand-name repair technician vary widely among manufacturers; in general, though, a manufacturer will require that you have (1) the ability and technical expertise to repair the equipment, (2) the necessary tools, and (3) an inventory of repair and replacement parts, which you will probably be required to purchase from the company.

Customers will expect you, as an authorized service person, to be able to repair their equipment, especially while it is still under warranty. They will expect you to act as their agent in dealing with the manufacturer, and to answer their questions.

Conversely, the authorizing company may be obliged to supply you with some assistance: technical literature, service manuals, and help in solving difficult or unusual problems, for example. You will be allowed to work on warrantied equipment, and you will be reimbursed by the manufacturer when you do so. As an authorized technician, you will probably get a better price on parts and tools from the manufacturers with whom you have authorization agreements.

Again, these arrangements vary among manufacturers.

To find out what they are, write to the service division of the company whose equipment you wish to repair. Check also with other repair firms in your area to find out how the arrangements work in actual practice.

A Small Warning

No matter what job you are considering, a small warning is in order here. If a manufacturer or retailer promises you hands-on training in the repair of computers, make sure you will really get that training. Talk to repair technicians already working for the company or retailer. "They promised I'd get the manufacturer's training program, but I've been here nearly a year and it hasn't happened" is a complaint of some new repair technicians. Make sure it won't be your complaint; check carefully before you take the job.

Working Papers

Take care, also, that you are suitably certified and licensed for the work you are undertaking. Most repair centers and retail computer outlets will tell you what credentials, if any, you need to work for them. But if you work on your own, you will have to find out for yourself.

Computer repair technicians are not specifically licensed in some states, and are presently operating in a "gray area." As the industry progresses, however, credentialing will likely become the rule, and requirements will probably resemble those presently in force for TV and radio repair.

Right now you or your employer will probably need a license to repair consumer products, at least. If you intend to make changes in wiring of homes or businesses, you will need an electrician's license; to qualify in Connecticut, for example, you need eight thousand hours of practical experience under the supervision of a licensed electrical contractor. To be a licensed television or radio service technician, you must generally serve an apprenticeship, take a state examination, and renew your license every year.

You need to know two things: (1) the credentials your state requires now, and (2) the credentials that are likely to be required in the future. You can get this information from your state licensing board, the department of higher education, your local technical or vocational school, and your local department of consumer protection. It's a good idea to get information from all of these sources, rather than relying on answers from just one person. Check and recheck the answers you get, resolving inconsistencies as best as you can, until you are sure you understand which licenses and credentials you need for the work you want to do.

You may also be interested in labor organizations; more to the point, they may be interested in you. Unions exist to protect their members from unfair competition, among other things. You can't just sail into an area and undercut the local prices without arousing some enmity.

The International Brotherhood of Electrical Workers and the United Electrical Radio & Machine Workers are just two of the unions that may be established in your locality. Find out who they are, what they do, what they require from you, and what they offer to their members. You may want to join. If the union is strong, it's possible that you will get no work until you do join. Check it out.

You Won't Be Lonely—Or Poor

Even if no computer ever broke down, work would exist for electronics specialists who are well versed in computers. For example, some printers require that word-processing programs be altered before the printer can support them. Some cannot print characters as fast as they are received; it is necessary to install a communications protocol, to tell the word-processing program to wait for the printer.

These chores, as well as installation of components and peripherals, require at least rudimentary knowledge of the electronics involved. Some users are able to make these installations on their own, but many cannot. They need technical support.

Once a system is installed, the owner may wish to use it for much more than standard information-processing tasks. A computer can function as a burglar or fire alarm, as a recorder of environmental conditions such as temperature and humidity, a telephone-answering machine, or as a remote, preprogrammed on/off switch for lights and other household and business appliances. Correctly wired and programmed, a home computer can convince burglars that someone is at home, and it can call the police if its "act" is not believed, or is ignored.

Most owners of home or business computers are not equipped to set up such a system. They don't know what peripherals to buy, or how to install them. They don't know how to connect their computers to other devices, nor can they insure that the wiring in their homes and businesses will support such installations safely. They need you to build their electronic cottages, and to repair them when things go wrong.

An electronics technician can serve as a consultant, too. "We bought a computer, but it doesn't do what we wanted it to do, so no one uses it" is a cry heard too often throughout the land. Whether customers wish to invest in their very first computers, or to expand systems they already own, they may need someone to translate the advertising for them—that is, to transform features of systems into solutions to their specific problems—and to advise them on the best ways to meet their needs. A knowledgeable technician can even offer a "package deal," visiting the customer's premises, learning about what the customer wants to do, buying the best equipment for the customer's needs, installing it, and making it compatible with the original system, if any. (For more on consulting, see Chapter 9.)

The Sky's the Limit

The need for technical support is not limited to homes and businesses. You can combine your other interests with your knowledge of computers and specialize in designing and building custom hardware for unusual tasks, or in combining standard components in new ways for special situations.

The lighting for many Broadway stage shows, for example, is now controlled by computer. Fuel-delivery systems for jet engines are designed by computer, as are the planes themselves; if you can design a system that simulates airflow around a jet aircraft, the Boeing Corporation wants to give you a lot of money.

Opportunities for computer specialists are limited only by their energy, knowledge, imagination, and technical skill. If you have reasonably nimble fingers and a nimble brain, this growing career opportunity may be for you.

PART III

CHAPTER 11

Time and a Half from the First Minute On

Let's start with a riddle: What's the difference between a hand-written holiday-card list, and one generated by a home computer?

Answer: Two hundred eighty hours, or more than five *thousand* dollars.

How? Let's assume you send out one hundred cards every year. You might spend eight hours a year addressing envelopes—which at a couple of hours per evening doesn't seem like much. But let's be optimistic, and assume you're going to do it every year for thirty-five years. (For simplicity's sake, we'll keep the size of your list constant.)

Eight hours per year times thirty-five years comes to 28Ø hours, or seven working weeks of your life.

Alternatively, imagine addressing those envelopes with your computer, using a printer equipped with a tractor feed, and envelopes tipped onto form-feed paper. You can print all those envelopes in about twenty minutes; over thirty-five years, you'll spend about twenty-three hours, including the time it takes to update your list.

Now you've got six and a half free weeks. What are you going to do with that gift of time?

Well, you might spend it printing greeting-card envelopes for other people. Your dentist, lawyer, accountant, and real estate agent probably send holiday cards to their clients, for example. What if you round up six professionals, each of whom sends two hundred cards per year, and offer to do it for them?

The first year you'll invest 40 hours typing in the names and addresses (we didn't count typing time for your list, since you'd have addressed those envelopes anyway). That year and every year thereafter, you'll spend about 5 hours printing the envelopes. Total time over thirty-five years is 175 hours. Let's add 10 hours of list-updating and other miscellaneous chores, and call it 185.

Let's say your clients supply the envelopes, and assume further that you charge the very reasonable sum of $25 for printing a batch of two hundred. Over the course of thirty-five years, you'll earn $5,250 on just 7 hours per year! That's nearly $30 an hour on time you would have spent anyway, and you've still got 95 free hours left over. If you take two more clients, you'll use 62 more hours and earn $1750 more, for a total of $7000. And you've still got 33 hours remaining.

Or, you could play *Space Invaders.* After all, it *is* your time—and your money.

And that's the point. Time is money. When you buy a home computer, you're investing money. The machine's efficiency gives you extra time, and furthermore increases the potential value of that time. In the case described above, it increases the value of time from $0 to $30 an hour!

This is called "a good return on your investment." It's the essence of capitalism, and the reason you bought your computer in the first place. You bought it to *use*—to help you do everything faster, easier, and better. You can make money on that saved time, but your return need not be measured only in money earned and saved. The computer can increase the intangible value of time, too—for example, by giving you more peace of mind, or more activities to pursue with your children.

Let's find some more ways to increase your return on the money you've spent. After that, we'll discuss exactly how to go about it.

Look at your checkbook. What does it tell you? Right away, it tells you how much money you've got. After much work from you, it tells you how much you've spent, and where you spent it. Essentially, it describes a single point on your financial timeline. That point is "right now."

It doesn't tell you how you arrived. It doesn't tell you where you're going. It says nothing at all about where you'd like to be, or how to get there. It doesn't supply the single most necessary element of your financial life: a plan.

Furthermore, it costs you time—around 12 hours per year, say, reconciling it with the bank's statement. Over thirty-five years, that's 420 hours, or if you are the $30-an-hour envelope printer from our earlier example, $12,600.

But let's not be greedy. Let's assume those envelopes earn us just $200 per year. What shall we do with the money?

Well, we could spend it on Christmas presents. Then the computer has increased our buying power. But isn't there some better way to handle that money? We'd like to find out, but it is laborious to calculate alternative financial plans on paper, and it's just so easy to spend the cash. After all, it's only $200.

Okay, let's spend it—and lose $34,000!

That's right. Invest $200 every year for thirty-five years in something that yields just 8 percent, and at the end of the years you will have over 34,000 bucks—before taxes, of course.

The formula for future value of an investment, by the way, is this: payment $\times$ $(((1+i\%)^{n})-1)/i\%$. To figure this without a computer spreadsheet, add 1 to the percentage of interest, raise the power to the total of the number of years you'll be investing, subtract 1, divide the result by the percentage of interest, and multiply by the amount of a single investment. Like this:

$$200 \times ((((1+.08)^{35})-1)/.08)$$

Simple, you say—I could have figured that out with a hand calculator. Sure, you could. But it's a lot easier with a computer spreadsheet, like this:

Al = \$200 B1 = .08 C1 = 35

The formula: $Al \times (((1+B1)^{c1})-1)/B1$.

On the computer screen, the SuperCalc spreadsheet with values and formula plugged in will look like Figure 4.

```
   | A  || B  || C  || D  || E  || F  || G  || H  |
 1| 200     .08     35      34463.36
 2|
 3|
 4|
 5|
 6|
 7|
 8|
 9|
10|
11|
12|
13|
14|
15|<       >
16|
17|
18|
19|
20|
v A15
Width:  9  Memory:28 Last Col/Row:D1       ? for HELP
 22>A1*(((1+B1)^C1)-1)/B1
```

Figure 4.

Let's suppose you scrape up an extra $50 per year and invest it, too. We change the value of A1 from $200 to $250, and the computer recalculates. The spreadsheet is shown in Figure 5.

Now at the end of thirty-five years you'll have \$43,000!

With your home computer and an electronic spreadsheet such as SuperCalc, you can construct alternative financial plans, choose the best one for your situation, and further increase your return on your computer investment. You can plan your budget, manage your investments, calculate the effects of inflation, and compare your goals with

```
   |  A   ||  B   ||  C   ||  D   ||  E   ||  F   ||  G   ||  H   |
  1| 25Ø      .Ø8       35      43Ø79.2Ø
  2|
  3|
  4|
  5|
  6|
  7|
  8|
  9|
 1Ø|
 11|<        >
 12|
 13|
 14|
 15|
 16|
 17|
 18|
 19|
 2Ø|
v All
Width:  9  Memory:28 Last Col/Row:D1       ? for HELP
 22>A1*(((1+B1)^C1)-1)/B1
```

Figure 5.

your current performance, making adjustments where necessary.

Unlike your checkbook, which only shows you where you are now, your computer offers a map of your whole financial terrain, as well as the tools you need to travel it safely and profitably.

So, you started with 28Ø hours, a computer, and a greeting-card list. You earned $7ØØØ on 247 of those hours, and you have 33 hours left. Add the 12 per year that you would have spent on that antiquated chore, balancing your checkbook. 12 × 35 = 42Ø hours, + 33 = 453 hours.

Remember: you'd have spent 28Ø hours addressing your own greeting cards, anyway. Your investment consists of the money you spent on the computer, software, and peripheral equipment. You now have more free hours than you started with, plus $7ØØØ, plus whatever you've earned by investing that $7ØØØ. Did you spend $12,ØØØ? Did you get

$34,ØØØ? Well, then, you have just earned nearly 2ØØ percent on your investment.

Not bad, and it's just the beginning.

Here are more ways to use your home computer, save time, and increase the monetary and intangible value of that time.

An Address Book Data File

Great-Aunt Millie would love to hear about your new baby, and Uncle Rob follows your son's Little League career. In fact, lots of people want to know the latest about your family. But your life revolves around 2:ØØ A.M. feedings and the baseball-practice car pool; you haven't got time to sit down and write fifty letters, each of which contains the same information. And those photocopied mass mailings do look tacky—if you send one, everyone will wonder who got the original.

Solution: Create a data file containing the names and addresses of all your friends and relatives. Compose your family newsletter, and use some sort of packaged merge-print program to insert the names, addresses, and other variable information. Each letter will be an original. You can also use a letter file to keep records on your correspondence: Who's heard from you lately, and more important, who hasn't?

Do you belong to social clubs, volunteer organizations, or lobbying campaigns? Your home computer will keep membership records, rosters of projects, and accounts for dues and fund drives. It will store and print the minutes of your meetings, generate press releases, and print leaflets for leaflet campaigns.

Do you have a political cause? A petition may affect the decisions of your government representative—but an avalanche of letters will do more. Create a data file from the names and addresses of your petition's signatories, then send the petition to the government official you want to influence. Ask each petitioner to sign the prepared letter and send it, too—to give your cause double clout.

Moving day is another occasion that requires sending out a lot of mail when you have little time. Again, merge-print to create a form letter, telling everyone of your new address and phone. You've already got all their names and addresses in the computer; just write your change-of-address notice and print it on stamped postcards. Time consumed: an hour at most.

Once you have moved, you can easily update your list of frequently called numbers and insert listings of new friends. No messy crossing out in an electronic address book!

All of these applications make use of a word-processing program with the merge-print feature. Some packages have other names for the feature, which merges a form letter with a list of variables: name, address, salutation, and so on. It works like this:

First, you write the letter, tagging the places where you want variable information inserted. See Figure 6.

```
May 29, 1983

&name&
&address&
&city&, &state& &zip&

Dear &salutation&,

     Well, I know it has been a long time since I've written,
&salutation&, but you can expect to hear more from me in the
future.

     Little Jimmy hit a home run the other day and the first
thing he said was "You've got to write and tell &salutation&!"

     I hope the weather is fine there in &city&.  I hear the
&state& legislature has made July 1 the official &state&
&salutation& holiday--enjoy it!

     We think of you often, &salutation&, and hope to hear from
you soon.


                                        &close&,
```

Figure 6. The form letter

Next, create the data file, as shown in Figure 7.

The program will merge them, resulting in Figure 8.

On the other hand, there may be things you'd like to

```
Don Wise,343 Main St,Mayberry,NC,11111,Grandpa,Love
Millie Ginger,100 Bigtop Rd,Warren,SD,44444,Aunt Millie,Love
Rob Roy,43 Hickory Ave,Lillyville,VT,22222,Uncle Rob,Cheers!
```

Figure 7. The data file

write down, yet keep entirely to yourself. No doubt your family is the most trustworthy group of people ever seen on earth; still, the allure of your little, leather-bound diary with its tin lock may be more than they can withstand.

A Very Private Diary

Use a word-processing program to write it, and hide it in plain sight under a dull-sounding file name. It's unlikely, for example, that anyone will want a casual glance at a file labeled "TAXTBLS.DTA."

Your Very Private file might be a good place to put your "in-box." Here's where you store notes, ideas, reminders—the things you would ordinarily jot down on small bits of paper and promptly lose. One of the great advantages to using a home computer is that it stores all that random information in one place. You can use it as an "accessory memory" for things you don't want to think about right now, but don't want to forget. Will you need to make travel reserva-

May 29, 1983

Rob Roy
43 Hickory Ave
Lillyville, VT 22222

Dear Uncle Rob,

Well, I know it has been a long time since I've written, Uncle Rob, but you can expect to hear more from me in the future.

Little Jimmy hit a home run the other day and the first thing he said was, "You've got to write and tell Uncle Rob!"

I hope the weather is fine there in Lillyville. I hear the VT legislature has made July 1 the official VT Uncle Rob holiday--enjoy it!

We think of you often, Uncle Rob, and hope to hear from you soon.

Cheers!

Figure 8. The merge-printed letter

tions, buy a birthday gift, or send a follow-up letter in the near future? Jot it down, and save it in your private memory jogger.

Other kinds of programs are available to manage other tasks around your home. The computer can't rake leaves, defrost the freezer, or clean the attic, but it can sort those tasks according to the time they will take to do.

An Electronic Job Jar

List all the chores around your house, estimating the time each one takes. With a database management program, you can assign chores randomly in a sort of household roulette. Or, simply create lists of similar-sized jobs with your word-processing program. Then, if you've got half an hour and want to choose a half-hour chore, you can call up the half-hour list, and pick a job from it. The Electronic Job Jar will save time by organizing your housework; it's also a great way to beat your kids' ''But I did it *last* time'' blues.

Another way to save money is to let the computer do your comparison shopping for you. This does take time, and is probably better suited to a cooperative buying project than to one family's needs.

A Household Money-Miser

You probably scan the paper for grocery specials already. Simply take the supermarket section of the paper to your computer terminal. List your household needs, and the advertised prices of those items at various outlets; then ask the computer to list the lowest "bid" on each item, together with the store offering the bid. Next sort the list, assigning each item to the store offering the best price. The result: a shopping list for each store you wish to visit. Next week, you'll simply update the list and sort again. You can also use the Money-Miser to decide whether a sale is worth a trip, since to justify a dollar's worth of gas you must save more than a dollar on the total spent at your destination.

When you do spend money, decide whether or not the expense is deductible and record it. Six months from now, you may not remember why you thought that bottle of pickled peppers was a legitimate business expenditure. Uncertain, you may decide against deducting it. Here is a way to eliminate a lot of uncertainties and save time and money.

A Tax Data File

You're already keeping your checkbook records in a computerized file, aren't you? Simply identify them by code as you make the entry. For example, M for medical; BE for business entertainment; S for sorry, not deductible; and so on. Note ambiguous items, justifying them as best you can.

When tax time comes around, just sort your list by category and you won't need so many aspirins (code aspirin M for medical, and keep your receipt!). Your accountant will appreciate you, and the IRS is more likely to ignore you (yes, that's what you want). An entry a day keeps the taxman away, and the Tax Data file makes it easy to keep good records.

Maintenance Diary

Someday, when the plastic widget falls out of your automobile, you'll be glad you can prove that you maintained that widget correctly, just as the warranty requires. The replacement widget, which now costs six hundred dollars, will come out of Enormous Car Corp.'s pocket, not out of yours. And how about that new freezer you bought? It started wheezing the day it arrived? Keep a diary of the troubles you have with it, and a list of the food that spoiled. Computerized documentation looks impressive in small-claims court.

Bill-Paying File

This file lists all your regular creditors by name, address, and your account number. It prints envelopes, too, for those creditors who are too cheap to provide them, and it keeps a running tally of your household expenditures. It eliminates forgotten payments, and tells you what it's costing each month just to live. You may be pleasantly surprised at the effectiveness of your recent cost-cutting strategy, or unhappily reminded that you *need* a strategy. Either way, with a computerized Bill-Paying file, you'll *know* where you stand.

The money you manage with your computer might not even be real—yet. It is generally accepted that, to become wealthy, you must increase your capital by investing it. The trouble is, of course, that if you don't know what you're doing you can lose a bundle on the stock market, where the small independent investor is at a tremendous disadvantage in terms of information and skill. You'll want a professional to manage your *real* investment portfolio, but there's no reason you can't get in on the excitement and learn a lot on your own, too.

A Ghost Portfolio

Start with an imaginary sum—say, $1ØØØ. Gather as much information as you can, make your "ghost" investment, then follow your gains and losses. How do you fare, compared with the rise and fall of the market? You can develop several strategies for investing your $1ØØØ and compare their performances.

Your home computer is a powerful tool for assessing potential investments; with already existing packaged software, you can test the profit potential of stocks and commodities before you buy or sell.

If you're investing real money, you may want real help. Dow Jones offers four software packages to help manage—and acquire—financial information. The Connector™ allows electronic access to financial data; the Market Analyzer™, Market Microscope™, and Market Manager™ allow storage and analysis of market information and market indicators, as well as portfolio accounting and control systems.

Steady losses may convince you to let the professionals invest for you, but consistent gains may release creativity and reveal a talent you never knew you had. Either way, you'll learn and have fun. And fun is value—more return on the money you spent for your computer—even if you lose an imaginary bundle on the market.

Here is another task for database management:

Medical Records

An accurate medical history on each member of your family may be invaluable should anyone suffer an accident or become ill. Include immunizations, allergies, drug reactions, any known exposures to toxic substances or to communicable diseases.

Should illness or injury strike, the Medical Records file can simplify complicated medication schedules; you can create a time sheet that tells exactly when to take what. Many printers allow you to adjust typeface and spacing; a large-print medication schedule confers independence on an ill or elderly person whose sight may be impaired.

When medications are changed, you can easily update the schedule and print the revision; when the patient is well, a final Congratulations! sheet may be in order. Just print zeros where medicine dosages appeared previously.

Another way to increase the value of your time is by increasing your security.

Computerized Home Security System

Your computer can generate the illusion that your house is occupied when you're away. It will turn lights, the TV and stereo, even the vacuum cleaner on and off as if you were home. You can randomize the on/off timer to avoid an obviously mechanical pattern. Furthermore, an opened door or window can trigger a tape-recording of a big dog—or a siren. Any penetration of your system can trigger an automatic call to the police, and activation of your smoke detector summons the fire department. Protecting your home and family from danger offers an excellent way to secure an intangible—but very real—return on your computer investment.

Your garden, of course, lies at the other end of the technical scale; there, a Rototiller may be the most elaborate machinery in use. If your "garden" happens to be forty thousand acres of prime bottomland, you may want to invest in packaged software for financial livestock planning, crop management, and marketing. Otherwise, you can use a simpler system.

A Garden Diary

Keep records of the types of seeds used, soil conditions, fertilization, strategies for pest control, and the amount of light and water your plants received. Record changes in your garden's yield from year to year, as you change methods.

Why search dozens of catalogues looking for a varietal whose name you've forgotten? In the "planning" section of your diary, note what you'd like to try next, and where it can be obtained. With the time you've saved, you can dig an asparagus bed. Your Garden Diary is a lasting record of your relationship with that little patch of earth, and it will improve your garden by showing you what works and what doesn't.

Now you've seen a few of the many things you can do with your home computer. But, you say, I can do most of those things already, with pencil and paper.

You're right, you can—slowly, less accurately, and with considerable effort. For example, let us assume that you receive $200 per year from an unknown benefactor. You want to know how much you'll have in thirty-five years if you invest it at 8 percent. You can repeat the same calculation thirty-five times, or you can plug the equation into your calculator. You can do it again and again, plugging in the varying interest rates and tax advantages for all your possible investments. Sharpen lots of pencils and gather up a big pile of scratch paper—and be sure you don't make any expensive mistakes in addition or multiplication!

Or, you can simply plug the numbers and the equations into your electronic spreadsheet. In a few minutes you'll have the bottom line on each potential investment.

That, in a nutshell, is the difference between working by hand and working with a computer. It works accurately, economically, and efficiently—just the way you want your home to run.

Now that you've saved money and time by putting a computer to work on your household tasks, we urge you to do one more thing: seize some of that saved time for yourself.

Think about it. You imagined buying a computer, you got up the nerve to go out and invest, and you learned how to run the thing. By making those smart moves, you've improved your family's health, happiness, and security, increased the learning and earning power of your household, and probably invested a few bucks in games and educational programs, too.

You deserve a reward. How about half an hour per day for yourself, every day? You could write that novel you've thought about; one page per day times 365 days equals one first draft. You could exercise, meditate, learn a language, or take a nap. You could learn a computer programming language, or start a home business.

Your computer can help you do *more,* in *less* time. By investing in it, you took control of a simple equation: time equals money, *or* whatever else you want it to equal—an exercise program, greater self-knowledge, a better relationship with your mate, your children, and your friends—anything *you* want to do.

So, the next time someone pooh-poohs the "silly idea" of sending out holiday cards by computer, just think about your happy relatives, your flourishing stock portfolio, your lush garden, and your safe, efficient household running smoothly along like a good Swiss watch. Think about the $34,000 you're making on that "silly idea."

Then, if you feel generous, give the pooh-pooher a copy of this book.

Or . . . just smile.

CHAPTER 12

Deep in the Heart of Taxes

Ah . . . the Ides of April. Birds singing in the trees, the smell of new-mown grass filling the air . . . and the Internal Revenue Service man, sharpening his knives, waiting to get his meathooks into what remains of your money.

We're going to outline how being a Very Small Business owner with a PC can cut down on the taxman's bite—and how you may actually be able to end up with more money, even while (technically) losing money on your VSB.

But first three caveats. The first is a disclaimer: While we have thoroughly researched this subject—one of the Internal Revenue Service's more readable publications is #587, "Tax Information on Operating a Business in Your Home"; you can order it for free—none of us are lawyers or tax accountants. What is in this chapter is the best information and advice we have available, but if you get bitten by the Internal Revenue Service shark, you're on your own.

The second caveat is this: When you're dealing with the IRS, you do not have a home computer, or a personal computer, or a PC—what you have is a "business microcomputer." Call it that; it may avoid trouble.

Which leads to the third, and most important, caveat. Don't be offended, but

You Need Professional Help

Although you won't need anyone to add up columns of numbers for you—use your spreadsheet and/or database program for that, which will save your accountant some time and trouble, and yourself some money—good, professional, personal tax advice from a competent tax accountant is invaluable.

While the Internal Revenue Service claims that an eighth-grader should be able to read and fill out their forms, that simply isn't so, particularly when you get into areas like depreciation, and Internal Revenue Service explanations like "for tax years beginning in 1982, you may choose to expense part of the cost of recovery property."

It's not just the unnecessarily opaque language; congressional action, or court decisions, or Internal Revenue Service policy can, at any time, change what you're allowed to do—and what you will get slapped with a fine and/or interest fees for doing. "Ignorance of the law is no excuse" is the Internal Revenue Service's secondary stock-in-trade. The primary one, of course, is fear.

While, at present, the Internal Revenue Service does operate a free tax advice service, that free advice can be very expensive—their "experts" get 2Ø percent of the *easy* questions wrong. (And, yes, you sure as anything do have to pay fines and interest, and/or spend some time in the slammer if you make a mistake while relying on bad advice from the Internal Revenue Service.) Besides, they're not working for you, no matter what the Civil Service Code says.

Once you become a VSB operator, you will absolutely, positively *have* to get professional tax advice. This may cost you up to a couple of hundred dollars per year; it will almost certainly save you far more than it costs.

And don't start looking for tax advice on April 14, either. You will save a lot of hassle *and money* by consulting your accountant well in advance.

Getting an Accountant

What if you don't already have an accountant? Get one.

Here's how. Look in the Yellow Pages for accountants who run their own, solo businesses, preferably out of their own homes. (Two reasons for this: (1) you don't want to help pay the overhead for a fancy, multiaccountant downtown office, and (2) an accountant operating out of his own home will be more than usually familiar with a lot of the deductions you should be taking—after all, he's taking most of the same ones.) Now start dialing.

Explain that you're a VSB operator who needs an accountant, and that you'd like to pick his or her brains for an hour. Offer to pay the accountant's standard fee for that hour. Almost invariably, the accountant will turn down your offer of payment (a lot of accountants are really nice people who spend far too much time jotting numbers in journals) and will end up giving you more than an hour's worth of time and advice (accountants like to talk—honest).

By the way, if the accountant doesn't have a computer yet, he'll probably want to pick your brains, too. You may be able to work out a trade, even pick up a bit of extra money doing some computerized bookkeeping for him. The electronic money machine should be kept humming. . . .

The key criteria in choosing an accountant, now that you've narrowed down the field, are competence—talk with a client or two—and compatibility. Your accountant is someone you should enjoy calling up with a question.

While you'll want him to fill out the rest of your Form 1040 (put the right number in the wrong place and you may be looking down the barrel of an audit), your accountant's main role is to advise you.

You need advice in four areas: Schedule C deductions, investment tax credits, retirement plans (Keogh plan, or ESOP), and incorporation. We'll take a look at each of these, the most important—and the one where you can do most of the work yourself—first.

Schedule C Deductions

Your first objective, come April 16 (that's the *latest* you want to start thinking about next year's taxes) is to plan on taking every deduction you can off Schedule C (Form 1040), Profit or (Loss) From Business or Profession (Sole Proprietorship). While you may have to settle for reducing your paper profit, the ideal thing to do is to get your Schedule C to show the largest loss—or "(Loss)," as the Internal Revenue Service would have it. That doesn't necessarily mean that you've really lost money, by the way. "Profit," in the tax business, can be a very plastic term.

Ideally, you will want to show a profit for only two out of every five years, managing your profit and expenses so that you can show a loss the other three. We're not talking about cheating here; rather, we're talking about legal ways to pay less tax.

You do this by taking deductions, and that's where the goodies start. As an accountant once said, "Once you go into business for yourself, your life is a deduction."

But *have* you gone into business for yourself? Yes, *we* know you have, but you've got to be able to persuade the Internal Revenue Service that what you're doing with your electronic money machine is business (in which case you can deduct all the goodies) as opposed to a hobby (in which *sigh* case you have to declare your net earnings on line 24 of your Form 1040 as "Other Income"; and there's no room on that tiny little line for all of the pretty deductions).

The simple, no-problem way to prove you're a business is to show that you've made a profit for two of the past five years.

That can be very difficult if you just started your VSB last January.

But businesses don't always make profits—ask the chairman of the board of TWA (and then duck). You can also prove you're a business by dazzling the Internal Revenue Service with paperwork, by showing through your records that you're not engaged in a hobby, that you're *trying* to turn a profit, that you are handling your business in a businesslike manner. This means you have to keep records, detailed records, of expenses and income.

Of course, you won't want to actually deal with your records on paper; it's too bulky. Use your DBMS, or invest in a tax-records program (ask your accountant which one to buy). Once you've logged a check or receipt into your database, just slip it into the shoebox or steamer trunk where you're going to keep that year's receipts, and don't worry about it—you should be able to handle it via database much more easily than by shuffling pieces of paper around.

This brings us to the Two Commandments of Schedule C deductions: "Thou shalt get receipts," and—whenever possible—"Thou shalt pay by a check drawn on thy business account." Which boils down to one commandment: *"Thou shalt get receipts."*

Engrave that on your wallet.

In general, you can deduct at least a portion of anything you spend on anything that is in any way related to your business. To wit:

Advertising. Off comes the cost of your Yellow Pages ad, plus any other sort of advertising you do. If you get imprinted pens—to be given out to clients, of course—take those off, too. Ditto business cards and the cost of hiring an art student to design your logo.

Bank service charges. Your accountant will probably advise you to open a separate business account for your VSB. Good—all the service charges for that account come off here. Rather than getting a NOW account, with its required minimum balance, you may be better off having a standard commercial account. It's deductible, after all. Ask your accountant.

Car expenses. As of this writing, the standard deduction for business use of a car is the actual cost of that use, or twenty cents per mile, whichever is greater. We suggest you go for the latter. It's easier to prove with the penciled log you'll keep in your glove compartment. The other method—regardless of whether or not it's accurate—may trigger an audit. And whether you're Vincent Teresa or Mother Teresa, you don't want to trigger an unnecessary audit.

Be sure to include all trips that are in any way related to your business, including trips to shop for your computer, or for some extra software. (Include the trip you took to the store to buy this book, of course.) Take a prorated portion of your auto insurance payments, too.

Commissions. If you use an agent, every penny you pay him or her comes off here.

Depreciation. This is one of the more complicated parts of your tax form. In its infinite wisdom, the government has decided that you can take part—or all—of the cost of investments you've made in your business as an expense.

It used to work like this—and it still does, for property put in service before January 1, 1981. Take the total cost of the property—your computer, for example. Figure out how long it will last you, and divide the price by that number of years. Each of those years, you depreciate the property by that much. That's called straight-line depreciation, and it used to be the most useful kind for VSB owners.

For most property placed in service after December 31, 1980, you use the Accelerated Cost Recovery System. An example: You buy a computer this year. You think—or claim—it will last five years. You deduct 15% of the cost the year the computer is placed in service, then 22%, 21%, 21%, and 21%.

You have another option, which the Internal Revenue Service calls "expensing." You treat the computer (plus computer stand, plus printer, plus filing cabinets, etc.) as a one-time expense, and deduct the whole thing the first year you put it into service. There are limits to how much "expensing" you can do (see **Investment Tax Credits,** below).

After you've finished deciding how to treat your computer and related property, you'll fill out Form 4562. A sample is shown in Figures 9 and 10.

Dues and publications. Anything you join, or buy to read, that does or may help you in your business comes off here. You need a daily newspaper, of course, to look at the want ads—someone may need the help of your electronic money machine—so deduct your subscription. And no, you don't have to buy a separate newspaper to read Dear Abby, or chuckle along with Garfield.

Are you a member of the Jaycees? Well, you'll make valuable business contacts there—deduct it. Computer mag-

Form **4562** (Rev. September 1982)
Department of the Treasury Internal Revenue Service (0)

Depreciation and Amortization

▶ See separate instructions.
▶ Attach this form to your return.

OMB No. 1545-0172
Expires 8/31/85
67

Name(s) as shown on return: JOHN SMITH
Identifying number: NA

Business or activity to which this form relates: J.S. ENTERPRISES - TERM PAPER TYPING

Part I Depreciation

Section A Election to expense recovery property (Section 179)

A. Class of property	B. Cost	C. Expense deduction

1 Total (not more than $5,000). Enter here and on line 8 (Partnerships—enter this amount on Schedule K (Form 1065)) . . . . .

Section B Depreciation of recovery property

A. Class of property	B. Date placed in service	C. Cost or other basis	D. Recovery period	E. Method of figuring depreciation	F. Percentage	G. Deduction for this year
2 Accelerated Cost Recovery System (ACRS) (See instructions):						
(a) 3-year property						
(b) 5-year property	COMPUTER-1/8/82	2554.90	5 YRS	PRE	15	383.23
	STAND-1/22/82	259.37	5 YRS	PRE	15	38.91
	CABINET-12/1/82	200.00	5 YRS	PRE	15	30.00
	PRINTER-12/31/82	2275.00	5 YRS	PRE	15	341.25
	PROGRAMS-1/8/82	645.00	5 YRS	PRE	15	96.75
(c) 10-year property						
(d) 15-year public utility property						
(e) 15-year real property—low-income housing						
(f) 15-year real property other than low-income housing						
3 Property subject to section 168(e)(2) election (See instructions):						
4 Total column G. Enter here and on line 9						890.14

See Paperwork Reduction Act Notice on page 1 of the separate instructions. Form **4562** (Rev. 9–82)

Figure 9. Form 4562 (front)

Form 4562 (Rev. 9–82) Page **2**

Section C Depreciation of nonrecovery property

A. Description of property	B. Date acquired	C. Cost or other basis	D. Depreciation allowed or allowable in earlier years	E. Method of figuring depreciation	F. Life or rate	G. Deduction for this year
5 Class Life Asset Depreciation Range (CLADR) System Depreciation ▶						
6 Other depreciation (See instructions):						
7 Total column G, Section C						
8 Enter amount from Section A, line 1 (Partnerships enter zero)						
9 Enter amount from Section B, line 4						890.14
10 Total—Add lines 7, 8, and 9. Enter here and on the Depreciation line of your return						890.14

Part II Amortization of property

A. Description of property	B. Date acquired	C. Cost or other basis	D. Amortization allowed or allowable in earlier years	E. Code section	F. Amortization period or percentage	G. Amortization for this year
Total column G. Enter here and on Other deduction or expense line of your return						

© U.S. GOVERNMENT PRINTING OFFICE 1982—O-363-359 23 188 5979

Figure 10. Form 4562 (back)

azines? Of course—you may want to upgrade your hardware or software. Your WordStar manual—deduct.

Please don't forget to deduct the cost of this book.

Freight. Ship anything anywhere for a business purpose, and it's deductible. Besides, an Express Mail or Federal Express envelope will impress the hell out of your client.

Insurance. You will, of course, want to insure your machine against theft or damage. Off it comes.

Interest on business indebtedness. If you've borrowed money to buy your machine or otherwise finance your VSB, deduct it.

This can be a very pretty deduction. If you have a straight life insurance policy that lets you borrow against its equity, you may choose to do that to buy or upgrade your computer. Deduct the interest.

Laundry and cleaning. If you use your three-piece suit or suited skirt *only* for business purposes, it's a uniform. (Be prepared to have many, many witnesses who will swear that you live in jeans and T-shirts the rest of the time.) Deduct the cleaning costs, and depreciate the suit. Ditto if you hire a cleaning service to clean your office—and if you hire a part-time cleaning person to clean your house or apartment, you can deduct a prorated portion of what you pay him or her. Use the same ratio as you do under **Rental on business property,** below.

Legal and professional services. Whatever you pay your accountant comes off here. If you need a will drawn up for business purposes, deduct the lawyer's fees.

Office supplies and postage. Buy stamps by the roll, not one at a time; pay by check, and deduct. Paper, disks, printer cleaning kits, ribbons, pens, pencils, envelopes, printer's bills, paper clips, file folders, the notebook you keep in your car to jot down business mileage, stamp pad, rubber stamps, ashtrays (not cigarettes—quit smoking), your coffee mug and coffeemaker (don't forget the filter cones, but don't *sigh* deduct your coffee), platens for your printer, Windex for your office windows—take them off.

Repairs. The entire cost of your service contract comes off here—you're paying for the repairs, even if you end up not needing them—plus any other repairs to your office. If your office chair breaks, take off the cost of fixing it.

Rental on business property. Of course, if you're renting your computer, that comes off here; ditto for a typewriter, outside office, copying machine, etc.

But the big deduction here is for an office in your home.

The government is of two minds on this. According to the Internal Revenue Service, you are only able to take a deduction for your "principal place of business"—that's the one where you make more money. If you make $20,000 a year at your regular job, but only $19,999.99 on your VSB, then—so they say—your regular job is your principal place of business, and you don't get to deduct for the office in your home.

But, the courts have held that if you have two businesses, you can have two principal places of business, and that if you're really running a VSB, instead of an MLH (Moderately Large Hobby), you can deduct your home office.

Again, here's where your accountant will be able to help you, should you be called in for an audit. He'll know the score, the Internal Revenue Service auditor will know that he knows the score. And that should settle that.

If you rent your home or apartment, you figure out your deduction as follows: Take the total floorspace of your home, excluding the bathrooms (they don't count). Now, figure out how much of your floorspace is *totally* devoted to your business (if you set up your computer on your kitchen table, it doesn't count). The ratio of the two figures is the portion of your rent that you can deduct in this category.

Let's take an example. Let's say that you rent a two-bedroom apartment for $500 a month, and you're using that second bedroom as an office. The living room measures thirty feet by twenty; the kitchen is fifteen by five; the master bedroom is ten by twelve; the second bedroom is ten feet square. And, just to make it more complicated, you have a tiny, three-feet-by-two foyer. You also have a huge bathroom, complete with Jacuzzi and hot tub. But don't count that; the Internal Revenue Service says that you don't have to, and if you did, you'd end up deducting a smaller portion of your rent.

Your total floorspace is nine hundred square feet and

your office floorspace is one hundred square feet; therefore, one-ninth of your rent is for business purposes.

Five hundred dollars times twelve months is $6000 per year. One-ninth of that is $666.66 (always round deductions down when you're dealing with the Internal Revenue Service—the fractional penny isn't worth an audit), so, in this case, you'd deduct that here.

Interesting. You'd be paying that $666.66 anyway, but now that you're a VSB operator, it's a deduction.

There is another way to figure your home-office deduction: just count your rooms. If you have five rooms, your office is one-fifth of your floorspace. Of course, if your office is tiny compared with your other rooms, you will gain a disproportionately large deduction, which the IRS will notice should you be called in for audit.

It's a bit more complicated if you own your own home, but not much more. First, you do the same sort of calculation as above, figuring out what proportion of your total floorspace is devoted to business. Then you deduct that ratio (one-ninth, in our example) from the amount of your mortgage bill that is interest, and sock it into the "Interest on Business Indebtedness" category of your Schedule C. Then do the same thing for the rest of your mortgage payments, or condo fees, or whatever.

Taxes. If you didn't buy your computer by mail, you paid state sales tax on it. Off it comes. In practice, you'll probably end up deducting the full price in the other category, including the tax. The Internal Revenue Service won't mind. But if you forget—or if you pay the tax separately—it comes off here. Ditto taxes on any other expenses.

If you own your home, you're paying property taxes. Deduct a portion of those (you'll deduct the rest of your property taxes on the Form 1040—don't save steps by deducting this fraction there), using the same ratio you calculated for the "Rental on Business Property" section.

Travel and entertainment. There are very few places where your accountant is better able to keep you out of trouble—while saving you money—than here. Basically, here you can deduct all business travel costs (other than auto mileage; that already came off) with a few curious exceptions. For example, if, while on a business trip, you buy yourself a meal, you can deduct it—but only if it's an overnight trip. (Internal Revenue Service figures that you would have had to eat anyway.) Or, if it's business entertainment. The three-martini lunch is deductible, right down to the olive.

For some reason, people on business trips very rarely eat alone, or just for the fun of it. There always seems to be a business purpose in grabbing a bite to eat. . . .

And, yes, business entertainment does include taking even a prospective client out to lunch at McDonald's and trying to wangle a deal over a Quarterpounder. McDonald's doesn't take checks—but they do give receipts. Save them, and note the client's name on the receipt.

Another bizarre exemption to the deduction rule involves conventions. (No matter what VSB you decide to go into, there is almost certainly a relevant convention or trade show somewhere—and during the winter, it'll probably be somewhere warm. Computer trade shows apply to everyone.) If the convention is in the U.S., go ahead and deduct your plane ticket, hotel bills, convention fees, meals, tips, taxis, and whatever you can show a receipt for. If, on the other hand, the convention is outside of the U.S., you must be able to show the Internal Revenue Service that the convention couldn't just as well have been held *in* this country.

If the convention is on a cruise ship, forget it. The Internal Revenue Service does not allow you to deduct the *Love Boat.*

Utilities and telephone. If you have a separate business phone line, deduct the whole thing. (But do buy your phone and depreciate it; it's cheaper that way.) If you use your home phone, you can deduct all your long-distance business calls, plus an appropriate proportion of your monthly service charge.

Deduct the same proportion of your other utilities as you do of your rent or mortgage payment.

Oh, you say you would have had to pay the electric bill for your former spare room anyway? Isn't that nice.

Wages. If you hire someone—and it may turn out that your VSB will grow to the point where you'll want to—you can deduct what you pay them, minus the jobs credit, if you're eligible, that you'll have already taken.

Other expenses. Generally, if it looks like a business expense, it is. Check with your accountant.

After you've done all this, your Schedule C will look something like Figure 11 (see page 181).

You may have noticed that many of these deductions are, or can be, for things that you would be doing anyway, or would want to do. As your VSB starts to save you money, you might find it easier to move into a larger apartment, with a bigger second bedroom; or take that trip to Los Angeles, cleverly timing it to coincide with the annual computer show; or dine out more often, taking a friend/prospective client along with you. If you can manage enough deductions, your VSB income will pull its full weight—or more—unhampered by the taxman's bite. You'll live better.

Which is what it's all about, no?

Now I've Got This Schedule C—What Do I Do with It?

If you show a loss, it's easy. Together with your accountant, figure out how much of that loss is for money that can be considered "at risk." Certainly, the money you've spent for your computer is at risk; probably, you should be able to consider a portion of the money you spend on rent and utilities as at risk.

With proper management, all of your loss is technically at risk. That's the reason that you've kept in touch with your accountant over the entire year; he can help you manage it right.

Then, on line 12 of your Form 1040, you put your loss in parentheses. You're going to subtract it from your other income, lowering the amount—and possibly the percentage—of income tax you'll have to pay on your regular earnings.

You then fill out your Schedule SE, noting happily that you don't have to pay any self-employment tax.

If you have a profit, it's only a little harder. Enter your profit on line 12, Form 1040, and fill out Schedule SE. If your paper profit is less than $400, smile—no SE tax. If it isn't, you pay the self-employment tax, which as of this writing is 9.35 percent of your profits. Notice the advantage of that over your regular income, which is subject to the FICA tax (granted, at a lower rate). Here, you're taking deductions *before* you have to pay tax; with FICA, it comes right off the top.

SCHEDULE C (Form 1040)
Department of the Treasury
Internal Revenue Service (0)

Profit or (Loss) From Business or Profession

(Sole Proprietorship)
Partnerships, Joint Ventures, etc., Must File Form 1065.
▶ Attach to Form 1040 or Form 1041. ▶ See Instructions for Schedule C (Form 1040).

OMB. No. 1545-0074
1982
08

Name of proprietor: JOHN SMITH
Social security number of proprietor: 999 99 9999

A Main business activity (see Instructions) ▶ TYPING TERM PAPERS ; product ▶ TYPED TERM PAPERS
B Business name ▶ J.S. ENTERPRISES
C Employer identification number: N/A
D Business address (number and street) ▶ 99 9TH ST
City, State and ZIP Code ▶ NEW HAVEN, CT 06511
E Accounting method: (1) [X] Cash (2) [ ] Accrual (3) [ ] Other (specify) ▶
F Method(s) used to value closing inventory:
(1) [ ] Cost (2) [ ] Lower of cost or market (3) [X] Other (if other, attach explanation) DOES NOT APPLY

	Yes	No
G Was there any major change in determining quantities, costs, or valuations between opening and closing inventory? If "Yes," attach explanation.		X
H Did you deduct expenses for an office in your home?	X	
I Did you operate this business at the end of 1982?	X	

J How many months in 1982 did you actively operate this business? ▶ 12

Part I Income

1 a Gross receipts or sales	1a	2590	00		
b Returns and allowances	1b		00		
c Balance (subtract line 1b from line 1a)				1c	2590 00
2 Cost of goods sold and/or operations (Schedule C–1, line 8)				2	
3 Gross profit (subtract line 2 from line 1c)				3	2590 00
4 a Windfall Profit Tax Credit or Refund received in 1982 (see Instructions)				4a	
b Other income				4b	
5 Total income (add lines 3, 4a, and 4b) ▶				5	2590 00

Part II Deductions

6 Advertising	67	75	25 Taxes (Do not include Windfall Profit Tax here. See line 29.)	53	37
7 Bad debts from sales or services (Cash method taxpayers, see Instructions)			26 Travel and entertainment	2195	00
			27 Utilities and telephone	428	57
8 Bank service charges	66	00	28 a Wages		
9 Car and truck expenses	341	12	b Jobs credit		
10 Commissions	22	50	c Subtract line 28b from 28a		
11 Depletion			29 Windfall Profit Tax withheld in 1982		
12 Depreciation, including Section 179 expense deduction (from Form 4562)	890	14	30 Other expenses (specify):		
			a XEROX COPYING	85	50
13 Dues and publications	175	00	b		
14 Employee benefit programs			c		
15 Freight (not included on Schedule C–1)			d		
16 Insurance	33	33	e		
17 Interest on business indebtedness	687	50	f		
18 Laundry and cleaning	20	00	g		
19 Legal and professional services	150	00	h		
20 Office supplies and postage	137	61	i		
21 Pension and profit-sharing plans			j		
22 Rent on business property	666	66	k		
23 Repairs	325	00	l		
24 Supplies (not included on Schedule C–1)			m		

31 **Total deductions** (add amounts in columns for lines 6 through 30m) ▶	31	([illegible]755	05)
32 Net profit or (loss) (subtract line 31 from line 5). If a profit, enter on Form 1040, line 12, and on Schedule SE, Part I, line 2 (or Form 1041, line 6). If a loss, go on to line 33	32		

33 If you have a loss, do you have amounts for which you are not "at risk" in this business (see Instructions)? [ ] Yes [ ] No
If you checked "No," enter the loss on Form 1040, line 12, and on Schedule SE, Part I, line 2 (or Form 1041, line 6).

For Paperwork Reduction Act Notice, see Form 1040 Instructions.

Figure 11. Schedule C

Figure 12 (page 183) is a sample Schedule SE, based on the Schedule C above.

Investment Tax Credits

Tax credits are even better than deductions. A deduction reduces your taxes in proportion to your tax bracket (i.e., the percent of taxes due on the last dollar you earned). To someone in the 25-percent bracket, a $100 deduction is worth $25 in savings.

A tax credit, however, reduces your taxes on a dollar-for-dollar basis, no matter what tax bracket you're in. A $100 tax credit cuts your taxes by $100, whether you're in the 15-percent bracket or the 50-percent bracket.

The question of ITCs gets complicated; it's related to depreciation. If you've decided to depreciate your computer over five years, you can take 10 percent of the price you paid for the computer as an ITC. However, if you do that, you must consider the cost of the computer (plus ancillary equipment, of course) as 5 percent less than it really was for the purpose of depreciation.

Alternatively, you can skip the ITC, and do what the Internal Revenue Service calls "expensing" the purchase price—taking the whole purchase price as a single deduction on one year's Form 1040. There are limits to expensing: for 1983, you can't expense more than $5000. For 1984 and '85, that goes up to $7500—after that, the sky's the limit. Unless Congress changes the laws, of course.

Which one should you do? The one that saves you more money. Calculating that depends not only on how much you made this year or last year, but on how much you will be making—at both your VSB and regular job—over the next few years. Make some guesses, then talk it over with your accountant. And not in early April; he'll be busy.

Figure 13 (page 184) shows how the ITC form might look.

Retirement Plans

Keogh plan. The basic retirement plan for the self-employed is the Keogh (pronounced *Kee*-oh) plan. While it's complicated beyond a nonaccountant's understanding, the basic notion is that you put up to 15 percent or $15,000 (whichever is smaller) of your VSB earnings in a special

SCHEDULE SE (Form 1040)
Department of the Treasury
Internal Revenue Service (0)

Computation of Social Security Self-Employment Tax

▶ See Instructions for Schedule SE (Form 1040).
▶ Attach to Form 1040.

OMB No. 1545–0074
1982
22

Name of self-employed person (as shown on social security card) JOHN SMITH

Social security number of self-employed person ▶ 999 99 9999

Part I **Regular Computation of Net Earnings from Self-Employment**

1 Net profit or (loss) from Schedule F (Form 1040), line 57 or line 90, and farm partnerships, Schedule K–1 (Form 1065), line 18b	1		
2 Net profit or (loss) from Schedule C (Form 1040), line 32, and Schedule K–1 (Form 1065), line 18b (other than farming). See instructions for kinds of income to report. **Note:** If you are exempt from self-employment tax on your earnings as a minister, member of a religious order, or Christian Science practitioner because you filed Form 4361, check here ▶ ☐. If you have other earnings of $400 or more that are subject to self-employment tax, include those earnings on this line	2	(3755	05)

Part II **Optional Computation of Net Earnings from Self-Employment**

Generally, this part may be used only if:

- Your gross farm profits were not more than $2,400, or
- Your gross farm profits were more than $2,400 and your net farm profits were less than $1,600, or
- Your net nonfarm profits were less than $1,600 and less than two-thirds (⅔) of your gross nonfarm income.

See instructions for other limitations.

3 Maximum income for optional methods	3	$1,600	00
4 Farm Optional Method—Enter two-thirds (⅔) of gross profits from Schedule F (Form 1040), line 31 or line 88, and farm partnerships, Schedule K–1 (Form 1065), line 18a, or $1,600, whichever is smaller	4		
5 Subtract line 4 from line 3	5		
6 Nonfarm Optional Method—Enter the smaller of two-thirds (⅔) of gross profits from Schedule C (Form 1040), line 7, and Schedule K–1 (Form 1065), line 18c (other than farming), $1,600, or, if you elected the farm optional method, the amount on line 5	6		

Part III **Computation of Social Security Self-Employment Tax** **SE**

7 Enter the amount from Part I, line 1, or, if you elected the farm optional method, Part II, line 4	7	00	00
8 Enter the amount from Part I, line 2, or, if you elected the nonfarm optional method, Part II, line 6	8	(3755	05)
9 Add lines 7 and 8. If less than $400, you are not subject to self-employment tax. Do not fill in the rest of the schedule	9	(3755	05)
10 The largest amount of combined wages and self-employment earnings subject to social security or railroad retirement tax for 1982 is	10	$32,400	00
11 a Total FICA wages from Forms W-2 and RRTA compensation — 11a			
b Unreported tips subject to FICA tax from Form 4137, line 9, or to RRTA tax — 11b			
c Add lines 11a and 11b	11c		
12 Subtract line 11c from line 10	12		
13 Enter the smaller of line 9 or line 12	13		
If line 13 is $32,400, fill in $3,029.40 on line 14. Otherwise, multiply line 13 by .0935 and enter the result on line 14		.0935	
14 Self-employment tax. Enter this amount on Form 1040, line 51	14		

For Paperwork Reduction Act Notice, see Form 1040 Instructions. 23 188 5979

U.S. GOVERNMENT PRINTING OFFICE: 1982—O-363-327

Figure 12. Schedule SE

Form **3468**
Department of the Treasury
Internal Revenue Service (0)

Computation of Investment Credit

▶ Attach to your tax return.
▶ Schedule B (Business Energy Investment Credit) on back.

OMB No. 1545-0155
1982
27

Name(s) as shown on return: JOHN SMITH | Identifying number: N/A

PART I.—Elections

A The corporation elects the basic or basic and matching employee plan percentage under section 48(n)(1) . . . . . ☐
B I elect to increase my qualified investment to 100% for certain commuter highway vehicles under section 46(c)(6) . . ☐
C I elect to increase my qualified investment by all qualified progress expenditures made this and all later tax years . . . ☐
Enter total qualified progress expenditures included in column (4), Part II ▶
D I claim full credit on certain ships under section 46(g)(3) (See Instruction B for details.) . . . . ☐

PART II.—Qualified Investment

1 Recovery Property		Line	(1) Class of Property	(2) Unadjusted Basis	(3) Applicable Percentage	(4) Qualified Investment (Column 2 × column 3)
Regular Percentage	New Property	(a)	3-year		60	
		(b)	Other	5934.27	100	5934.27
	Used Property	(c)	3-year		60	
		(d)	Other		100	
§48(q) Election to Reduce Credit (instead of adjusting basis) FY 1982–83 filers only (see instr.)	New Property	(e)	3-year		40	
		(f)	Other		80	
	Used Property	(g)	3-year		40	
		(h)	Other		80	

2 Nonrecovery property—Enter total qualified investment (See instructions for line 2) . .	2	
3 New commuter highway vehicle—Enter total qualified investment (See Instruction D(2)) .	3	
4 Used commuter highway vehicle—Enter total qualified investment (See Instruction D(2)) .	4	
5 **Total qualified investment in 10% property**—Add lines 1(a) through 1(h), 2, 3, and 4 (See instructions for special limits)	5	5934.27
6 Qualified rehabilitation expenditures—Enter total qualified investment for:		
a 30-year-old buildings	6a	
b 40-year-old buildings	6b	
c Certified historic structures (Enter the Dept. of Interior assigned project number)	6c	
7 Corporations checking election box A above—add lines 5, 6a, 6b, and 6c . . 7		

PART III.—Tentative Regular Investment Credit

8 10% of line 5	8	593.27
9 15% of line 6a	9	
10 20% of line 6b	10	
11 25% of line 6c	11	
12 Corporations checking election box A (See Instruction D(1))—		
a Basic 1% credit—Enter 1% of line 7 (1982–83 fiscal-year filers, see instructions for line 12) . . .	12a	
b Matching credit (not more than 0.5%)—Allowable percentage times adjusted line 7 (attach schedule) .	12b	
13 Credit from cooperative—Enter regular investment credit from cooperatives	13	
14 Current year regular investment credit—Add lines 8 through 13	14	
15 Carryover of unused credits	15	
16 Carryback of unused credits	16	
17 Tentative regular investment credit—Add lines 14, 15, and 16	17	

PART IV.—Tax Liability Limitations

18 a Individuals—From Form 1040, enter tax from line 38, page 2, plus any additional taxes from Form 4970 b Estates and trusts—From Form 1041, enter tax from line 26a, plus any section 644 tax on trusts . c Corporations (1120 filers)—From Form 1120, Schedule J, enter tax from line 3 . d Other organizations—Enter tax before credits from return	18	
19 a Individuals—From Form 1040, enter credits from lines 41 and 42 of page 2 . . b Estates and trusts—From Form 1041, enter any foreign tax credit from line 27a . c Corporations (1120 filers)—From Form 1120, Schedule J, enter any foreign tax credit from line 4(a), plus any possessions tax credit from line 4(f) . . . . d Other organizations—Enter any foreign or possessions tax credit	19	
20 Income tax liability as adjusted (subtract line 19 from line 18)	20	
21 a Enter smaller of line 20 or $25,000. See instruction for line 21	21a	
b If line 20 is more than $25,000—Enter 90% of the excess	21b	
22 Regular investment credit limitation—Add lines 21a and 21b	22	
23 Allowed regular investment credit—Enter the smaller of line 17 or line 22	23	
24 Business energy investment credit limitation—Subtract line 23 from line 20	24	
25 Business energy investment credit—From line 14 of Schedule B (Form 3468)	25	
26 Allowed business energy investment credit—Enter smaller of line 24 or line 25 . . .	26	
27 Total allowed regular and business energy investment credit—Add lines 23 and 26. Enter here and on Form 1040, line 43; Schedule J (Form 1120), line 4(b), page 3; or the proper line on other returns . .	27	

For Paperwork Reduction Act Notice, see separate instructions. Form **3468** (1982)

Figure 13. ITC form

bank account, stock account, or money-market fund, and pay no taxes on that money or the interest it earns until you retire, and start drawing it out. At that time, presumably, you will be in a lower tax bracket, and the Internal Revenue Service will be taking a smaller bite of a larger sum (remember, it's earning tax-free interest all the while).

Alternately, you can deduct the amount you do and have to invest in order to get a specific benefit at retirement age.

Confusing? If you'd like to be further confused, send away for Internal Revenue Service Publication 560, "Tax Information on Self-Employed Retirement Plans."

On the other hand, an accountant who knows you and is interested in your future well-being can help you decide what will work best for you, and how to get the feds to let you do it.

ESOP. This stands for Employee Stock Option Plan, a legal scam for corporations. It really isn't a retirement plan, although on paper it looks like one. It is, as we said, a scam, but it is a legitimate one—which means that the Internal Revenue Service will, at present, let you get away with it. That may change, of course (see caveat #1, at the beginning of this chapter).

It works like this: with an ESOP, your corporation (you *must* be incorporated to set one up) contributes shares of its stock to a retirement plan for its employee (that's you). The stock doesn't have a real value; you get to decide what the value of the paper you give yourself is, up to 15 percent of the salary you're paying yourself as an employee of your corporation.

While you're busy giving stock to yourself, your corporation takes the "value" of the distributed stock as a deduction—in effect, by shuffling paper around, you cut down your corporation's paper profits. And, therefore, pay less tax.

Eventually, of course, you'll run out of stock. You just issue some more, and start shuffling the paper again.

Notice: Other than the money you're paying your accountant and lawyer to set this up, no money is really changing hands.

Eventually, of course, you'll retire and, as with the

Keogh, the value of the stock will be taxable. But, in the interim, you've had the saved tax money to play with (that's you-the-corporation, not you-your-own-employee), and you'll be taxed at your lower, retirement rate.

The difference between an ESOP and a real retirement plan is money: in other retirement plans, you have to put some somewhere in order to qualify for the tax breaks; with ESOP, you just keep the paper flowing.

ESOP brings up an obvious subject:

Incorporation

As with most other topics mentioned in this chapter, for a VSB owner, incorporation involves shuffling paper around for the purpose of saving money. Possibly, a lot of money.

With incorporation, the piles of paper bring an added benefit: limited liability. If you incorporate—either regular or subchapter S incorporation—you can be sued for what you do in your VSB only to the limits of the assets of your corporation. Your house, personal bank account, car, and collection of antique riding crops are safe.

Also, your ability to play around—legally—with paper profits and retirement benefits goes up. That cuts down on your tax bill. ESOP is one example; your ability to deduct the cost of your health insurance is another. You may also find it easier to buy some things wholesale (some suppliers sell "to the trade only") or at a corporate discount.

There are, alas, drawbacks to incorporating. If you thought that the mass of paperwork and records you have to keep for Schedule C is a tad large, you'll find it massive for a corporation. You will certainly pay more taxes—although you will pay less tax.

You won't be able to mix-and-match your personal money and your corporate money; you'll have to be careful about how you pay yourself and when, as well as which checkbook you use to pay which portion of the utility bill.

You'll also have to get a lawyer, as well as an accountant.

And you're more likely to run into hassles with the Internal Revenue Service. The taxman will want to prove that you have no legitimate reason for forming a corporation—if you can't prove that you do, he can disallow the whole thing as a tax dodge.

That's where the traps *start.*

So why bother? Because you can end up paying significantly less tax. If you're making more than $15,000 or so per year from your VSB, the benefits might amount to enough to justify the hassle. Talk it over with your accountant.

Subchapter S incorporation. This is sort of a bastard hybrid between standard incorporation and a sole proprietorship. With this sort, you pass along your corporation's profits and losses directly from the corporation to yourself —without worrying about whether the taxman will try to disallow your corporation on the grounds that your salary is too high or too low.

Putting It All Together

Our fictitious VSB owner's Form 1040 might look like Figures 14 and 15 (pages 188–189).

As you read over his various forms, you'll notice that his VSB has paid off quite well, despite the fact that he is still making loan payments for his computer. He's traveling a lot, eating out often and well—and, in fact, paying less tax than he otherwise would.

Can your form look like this? Quite possibly.

One last time: Talk it over with your accountant.

Form **1040** Department of the Treasury—Internal Revenue Service
U.S. Individual Income Tax Return **1982** (0)

For the year January 1–December 31, 1982, or other tax year beginning , 1982, ending , 19 . OMB No. 1545-0074

Use IRS label. Otherwise, please print or type.	Your first name and initial (if joint return, also give spouse's name and initial): JOHN	Last name: SMITH	Your social security number: 999 99 9999
	Present home address (Number and street, including apartment number, or rural route): 99 9th ST.,		Spouse's social security no.
	City, town or post office, State and ZIP code: NEW HAVEN CT 06511	Your occupation ▶ Spouse's occupation ▶	

Presidential Election Campaign ▶ Do you want $1 to go to this fund? . . . Yes No. If joint return, does your spouse want $1 to go to this fund? . . . Yes No. Note: Checking "Yes" will not increase your tax or reduce your refund.

Filing Status — Check only one box. For Privacy Act and Paperwork Reduction Act Notice, see Instructions.

1 ☐ Single
2 ☐ Married filing joint return (even if only one had income)
3 ☐ Married filing separate return. Enter spouse's social security no. above and full name here ▶
4 ☐ Head of household (with qualifying person). (See page 6 of Instructions.) If the qualifying person is your unmarried child but not your dependent, enter child's name ▶
5 ☐ Qualifying widow(er) with dependent child (Year spouse died ▶ 19). (See page 6 of Instructions.)

Exemptions — Always check the box labeled Yourself. Check other boxes if they apply.

6a ✓ Yourself ☐ 65 or over ☐ Blind — Enter number of boxes checked on 6a and b ▶ 1
b ☐ Spouse ☐ 65 or over ☐ Blind
c First names of your dependent children who lived with you ▶ — Enter number of children listed on 6c ▶ 0
d Other dependents:

(1) Name	(2) Relationship	(3) Number of months lived in your home	(4) Did dependent have income of $1,000 or more?	(5) Did you provide more than one-half of dependent's support?

Enter number of other dependents ▶ 0
e Total number of exemptions claimed . . . Add numbers entered in boxes above ▶ 1

Income — Please attach Copy B of your Forms W-2 here. If you do not have a W-2, see page 5 of Instructions. Please attach check or money order here.

7	Wages, salaries, tips, etc.	7	12897 50
8	Interest income (attach Schedule B if over $400 or you have any All-Savers interest)	8	22 91
9a	Dividends (attach Schedule B if over $400) ...., 9b Exclusion		
c	Subtract line 9b from line 9a	9c	
10	Refunds of State and local income taxes (do not enter an amount unless you deducted those taxes in an earlier year—see page 9 of Instructions)	10	
11	Alimony received	11	
12	Business income or (loss) (attach Schedule C) ▶	12	(3755 05)
13	Capital gain or (loss) (attach Schedule D)	13	
14	40% capital gain distributions not reported on line 13 (See page 9 of Instructions)	14	
15	Supplemental gains or (losses) (attach Form 4797)	15	
16	Fully taxable pensions, IRA distributions, and annuities not reported on line 17	16	
17a	Other pensions and annuities. Total received 17a		
b	Taxable amount, if any, from worksheet on page 10 of Instructions	17b	
18	Rents, royalties, partnerships, estates, trusts, etc. (attach Schedule E)	18	
19	Farm income or (loss) (attach Schedule F) ▶	19	
20a	Unemployment compensation (insurance). Total received 20a		
b	Taxable amount, if any, from worksheet on page 10 of Instructions	20b	
21	Other income (state nature and source—see page 10 of Instructions) ▶	21	
22	**Total income.** Add amounts in column for lines 7 through 21 ▶	22	9165 36

Adjustments to Income (See Instructions on page 11)

23	Moving expense (attach Form 3903 or 3903F)	23	
24	Employee business expenses (attach Form 2106)	24	
25	Payments to an IRA. You must enter code from page 11 (......)	25	1934 63
26	Payments to a Keogh (H.R. 10) retirement plan	26	
27	Penalty on early withdrawal of savings	27	77 50
28	Alimony paid	28	
29	Deduction for a married couple when both work (attach Schedule W)	29	
30	Disability income exclusion (attach Form 2440)	30	
31	**Total adjustments.** Add lines 23 through 30. ▶	31	2012 13

Adjusted Gross Income

32	**Adjusted gross income.** Subtract line 31 from line 22. If this line is less than $10,000, see "Earned Income Credit" (line 62) on page 15 of Instructions. If you want IRS to figure your tax, see page 3 of Instructions ▶	32	7153 23

*U.S. GOVERNMENT PRINTING OFFICE 1982 363-300

Figure 14. Form 1040 (front)

Form 1040 (1982) Page **2**

Tax Computation (See Instructions on page 12)

33	Amount from line 32 *(adjusted gross income)*	33	7153 23
34a	If you itemize, complete Schedule A (Form 1040) and enter the amount from Schedule A, line 30	34a	
	Caution: If you have unearned income and can be claimed as a dependent on your parent's return, check here ▶ ☐ and see page 12 of the Instructions. Also see page 12 of the Instructions if: ● *You are married filing a separate return and your spouse itemizes deductions, OR* ● *You file Form 4563, OR* ● *You are a dual-status alien.*		
34b	If you do not itemize, complete the worksheet on page 13. Then enter the allowable part of your charitable contributions here	34b	
35	Subtract line 34a or 34b, whichever applies, from line 33	35	
36	Multiply $1,000 by the total number of exemptions claimed on Form 1040, line 6e	36	1000 00
37	Taxable Income. Subtract line 36 from line 35	37	6153 23
38	Tax. Enter tax here and check if from ☑ Tax Table, ☐ Tax Rate Schedule X, Y, or Z, or ☐ Schedule G	38	556 00
39	Additional Taxes. (See page 13 of Instructions.) Enter here and check if from ☐ Form 4970, ☐ Form 4972, ☐ Form 5544, or ☐ section 72 penalty taxes	39	00 00
40	**Total.** Add lines 38 and 39 ▶	40	556 00

Credits (See Instructions on page 13)

41	Credit for the elderly *(attach Schedules R&RP)*	41			
42	Foreign tax credit *(attach Form 1116)*	42			
43	Investment credit *(attach Form 3468)*	43	593 43		
44	Partial credit for political contributions	44			
45	Credit for child and dependent care expenses *(attach Form 2441)*	45			
46	Jobs credit *(attach Form 5884)*	46			
47	Residential energy credit *(attach Form 5695)*	47			
48	Other credits—see page 14 ▶	48			
49	**Total credits.** Add lines 41 through 48			49	
50	**Balance.** Subtract line 49 from line 40 and enter difference (but not less than zero) ▶			50	00

Other Taxes (Including Advance EIC Payments)

51	Self-employment tax *(attach Schedule SE)*	51	
52	Minimum tax *(attach Form 4625)*	52	
53	Alternative minimum tax *(attach Form 6251)*	53	
54	Tax from recapture of investment credit *(attach Form 4255)*	54	
55	Social security (FICA) tax on tip income not reported to employer *(attach Form 4137)*	55	
56	Uncollected employee FICA and RRTA tax on tips *(from Form W–2)*	56	
57	Tax on an IRA *(attach Form 5329)*	57	
58	Advance earned income credit (EIC) payments received *(from Form W–2)*	58	
59	**Total tax.** Add lines 50 through 58 ▶	59	00

06

Payments Attach Forms W–2, W–2G, and W–2P to front.

60	Total Federal income tax withheld	60	1934 63		
61	1982 estimated tax payments and amount applied from 1981 return	61			
62	Earned income credit. If line 33 is under $10,000, see page 15 of Instructions	62			
63	Amount paid with Form 4868	63			
64	Excess FICA and RRTA tax withheld (two or more employers)	64			
65	Credit for Federal tax on special fuels and oils *(attach Form 4136)*	65			
66	Regulated Investment Company credit *(attach Form 2439)*	66			
67	**Total.** Add lines 60 through 66 ▶			67	1934 63

Refund or Amount You Owe

68	If line 67 is larger than line 59, enter amount **OVERPAID** ▶	68	1934 63
69	Amount of line 68 to be **REFUNDED TO YOU** ▶	69	1934 63
70	Amount of line 68 to be applied to your 1983 estimated tax ▶ 70		
71	If line 59 is larger than line 67, enter **AMOUNT YOU OWE.** Attach check or money order for full amount payable to Internal Revenue Service. Write your social security number and "1982 Form 1040" on it. ▶ (Check ▶ ☐ if Form 2210 (2210F) is attached. See page 16 of Instructions.) ▶ $	71	

Please Sign Here

Under penalties of perjury, I declare that I have examined this return, including accompanying schedules and statements, and to the best of my knowledge and belief, it is true, correct, and complete. Declaration of preparer (other than taxpayer) is based on all information of which preparer has any knowledge.

▶ John Smith — Your signature | 1/9/83 — Date | ▶ Spouse's signature (if filing jointly, BOTH must sign)

Paid Preparer's Use Only

Preparer's signature ▶ | Date | Check if self-employed ▶ ☐ | Preparer's social security no.

Firm's name (or yours, if self-employed) and address ▶ | E.I. No. ▶ | ZIP code ▶

Figure 15. Form 1040 (back)

PART IV

SOURCES

Sources

This field is so alive that it seems like every time we visit a store we find a new book, magazine, software package, or system. Which is absolutely wonderful—except when it comes time to compile, for publication six months later, a comprehensive list of what's available to you, the computer owner. . . .

So we've compromised. We've listed *some* of what's out there. We do not claim to have all of it, or even most of it. Quite simply, there's too much of it.

We've deliberately included resources for specialists as well as for hobbyists—because if your VSB takes off, you'll want to hone your skills even more.

If you're interested in learning more about anything mentioned in the following pages, drop a line to the address given, or call the phone number, and ask the people who know it best. One warning, though: Most of the WATS (1-8ØØ) numbers given here are *not* good in the companies' home states. But Directory Assistance should be able to help.

Good luck!

Books

Title	Author	Publisher
1983 Components Handbook	Western Digital Corporation	Western Digital Corporation
Analytical Engine: Computers—Past, Present and Future, The	Bernstein, Jeremy	William Morrow & Co.
Assemblers, Compilers, and Program Translation	Calingsgert, Peter	Computer Science Press
Basic Computer Programs for the Home	Sternberg, Charles	Hayden Book Co.
Be a Computer Literate	Ball, Marion J., and Charp, Sylvia	Creative Computing
Before You Buy a Computer	Meilach, Dona	Crown Publishers
Beginner's Guide to Computers and Microprocessors—With Projects, A	Adams, C. K.	TAB Books
Beginner's Guide to Home Computers	Grosswirth, Marvin	Doubleday & Co.
Beginner's Manual for the PASCAL System, The	Bowles, Ken	McGraw-Hill Book Co.
Benchmarking: Computer Evaluation and Measurement	Benwell, Nicholas, ed.	Hemisphere Publishing
Best of Byte, The, Vol. 1	Ahl, David H., and Helmers, C. eds.	Creative Computing
Best of Creative Computing, Vol. 3	Ahl, David H., and Green, Burchenal, eds.	Creative Computing
Book of Apple Computer Software, The	Sadlier, J., and Stanton, J.	Addison-Wesley Publishing Co.
Build Your Own Z-8Ø Computer	Ciarcia, Stephen	McGraw-Hill Book Co.
Business Information Processing with Basic	Struble, George	Addison-Wesley Publishing Co.
CAI Sourcebook	Burke, Robert	Petrocelli Books
CBM Professional Computer Guide	Osborne, Adam, et al	Osborne/McGraw-Hill

Title	Author	Publisher
CP/M DiskGuide	Ingraham, Curtis	Osborne/McGraw-Hill
CP/M Word Processing	Que Corporation	Que Corporation
CRT Controller Handbook, The	Kane, Gerry	Osborne/McGraw-Hill
Careers in Computers	Ray, Jo A.	Lerner Books
Careers in Computers and Data Processing	McDaniel, Herman	Petrocelli Books
Chip Mitchell: The Case of the Stolen Computer Brains	D'Ignazio, Fred	E. P. Dutton
Ciarcia's Circuit Cellar	Ciarcia, Stephen	McGraw-Hill Book Co.
Complete Home Video Handbook, The	Dunton, Mark, and Owen, David	Random House
Components of Computers	Mazda, F. F.	State Mutual Books
Computer Anatomy for Beginners	Ouverson, Marlin	Reston Publishing Co.
Computer Awareness Book	Spencer, Donald D.	Camelot Publishing Co.
Computer Careers: Where the Jobs Are and How to Get Them	Consumer Guide Editors	Fawcett Books
Computer Chess	Levy, David	John Wiley & Sons
Computer Dictionary	Sippl, C. J., and Sippl, Roger	Howard W. Sams & Co.
Computer Dictionary for Everyone	Spencer, Donald	Charles Scribner's Sons
Computer Fundamentals for Nonspecialists	Vies, Joseph M.	American Management
Computer Graphics with Twenty-Nine Ready-to-run Programs	Chance, David	TAB Books
Computer People	Angus, Anne D.	Transatlantic Art
Computer Power and Human Reason: From Judgment to Calculation	Weizenbaum, Joseph	W. H. Freeman & Co.
Computer Programs in Science and Engineering	Gilder, Jules H.	Hayden Book Co.

Title	Author	Publisher
Computer Quiz Book, The	Spencer, Donald D.	Camelot Publishing Co.
Computer Survival Handbook, The	Woodbridge, Susan, and London, Keith	Gambit
Computer-Aided Design	Kaplinsky, Raphael	Macmillan Publishing Co.
Computer-Aided Information Retrieval	Wessel, Andrew E.	R. E. Krieger Publishing Co.
Computerist's Handy Manual	Hallmark, Clayton	TAB Books
Computers—How to Break into the Field	Carron, L. Peter	Liberty Press
Computers and Privacy in the Next Decade	Hoffman, Lance J., ed.	Academic Press
Computers for Everybody	Willis, Jerry, and Miller, Merl	Dilithium Press
Computing Systems Reliability	Anderson, T., and Randell, B.	Cambridge University Press
Data Structures and PL-1 Programming	Augenstein, Moshe	Prentice-Hall
Design of Operating Systems for Small Computer Systems, The	Kaisler, Stephen H.	John Wiley & Sons
Design of Well-Structured and Correct Programs	Alagic S., and Arbib, M. A.	Springer-Verlag
Devil's DP Dictionary, The	Kelly-Bootle, Stan	McGraw-Hill Book Co.
Electronic Cottage, The	Deken, Joseph	William Morrow & Co.
Electronic Money Machine, The	Haven Group, The	Avon Books
Essentials of COBOL Programming: A Structural Approach	Pitts, Gerald N., and Bateman, B.	Computer Science Press
Executive Guide to WordStar	Massie, Philip E.	Culver City Canon Co.
Fun with Computers and Basic	Spencer, Donald D.	Camelot Publishing Co.
Game Playing with Computers	Spencer, Donald D.	Hayden Book Co.
Giant Book of Computer Software, The	Seventy-Three Magazine Editors	TAB Books

Title	Author	Publisher
Global Stakes: The Future of High Technology in America	Botkin, James, et al	Ballinger Publishing Co.
Guide for Software Entrepreneurs, A	Frank, A.	Prentice-Hall
Guide to Reference Sources in the Computer Sciences	Carter, Ciel	Macmillan Publishing Co.
Handbook of Problem Solving, The	Andriole, Stephen J.	Petrocelli Books
Home Computers: A Beginner's Glossary and Guide	Miller, Merle, and Sippl, Charles	Dilithium Press
How to Break into Data Processing	Sessions, Laura Steibel	Prentice-Hall
How to Build a Computer-Controlled Robot	Loofbourrow, Tod	Hayden Book Co.
How to Buy and Use Minicomputers and Microcomputers	Barden, William, Jr.	Howard W. Sams & Co.
How to Choose Your Small Business Computer	Birnbaum, Mark, and Sickman, John	Addison-Wesley Publishing Co.
How to Computerize Your Small Business	Cohen, Jules, and McKinney, C.	Spectrum Books
How to Debug Your Personal Computer	Huffman and Bruce	Reston Publishing Co.
How to Design, Build and Program Your Own Working Computer	Haviland, Robert P.	TAB Books
IBM PC DiskGuide	White, David	Osborne/McGraw-Hill
IBM/PC Guide, The	Kelley, James E., Jr.	Banbury Books
Interactive Videotext	Chorafas, Dimitris	Dilithium Press
Introduction to Interactive Computer Graphics	Scott, Joan E.	John Wiley & Sons
Introduction to Programming with ESP and Pascal	Tucker, Allen B., Jr.	Holt, Rinehart & Winston
Introduction to the Z8Ø Microcomputer	Khambata, Adi J.	John Wiley & Sons

Title	Author	Publisher
Kids and Computers: The Parents' Microcomputer Handbook	Galanter, Eugene	Perigee Books
Kids and the Apple	Carlson, Edward H.	Reston Publishing Co.
Law and the Computer	Gemignani, Michael	CBI Publishing Co.
Layperson's Guide to Personal Computing	Peterson, Dale	Petrocelli Books
Microcomputer Uses in Small Business	Jackson, John K.	Datamasters
Microcomputer Workbook	Poirot, James, and Retzlaff, Don	Sterling Swift
Microprocessor Architecture and Programming	Leahy, William F.	John Wiley & Sons
Microprocessor and Microcomputer Data Digest	Buchsbaum, W. H., et al	Reston Publishing Co.
Microprocessors for Management: CAD, CAM, and Robotics	Chorafas, Dimitris N.	Petrocelli Books
Microsoft Basic Decoded and Other Mysteries	Farvour, James	IJG Inc.
Mind Appliance, The	Lewis, T. G.	Hayden Book Co.
More Basic Computer Games	Ahl, David	Creative Computing
Mouse: A Language for Microcomputers	Grogono, Peter	Petrocelli Books
Nailing Jelly to a Tree	Willis, Jerry, and Danley, W., Jr.	Dilithium Press
Online Reference and Information Retrieval	Palmer, Roger C.	Libraries Unlimited, Inc.
PET-CBM Personal Computer Guide	Osborne, Adam	Osborne/McGraw-Hill
Payroll with Cost Accounting—CBASIC	Poole, Lon, et al	Osborne/McGraw-Hill
Peanut Butter and Jelly Guide to Computers	Willis, Jerry	Dilithium Press
Personal Computer Book, The	McWilliams, Peter	Ballantine Books
Personal Computers Handbook	Buchsbaum, Walter	Howard W. Sams & Co.

Title	Author	Publisher
Personal Microcomputing in the Corporate Environment	Advanced Management Research, Inc.	AMR, Inc.
Playing the Stock and Bond Market with Your Personal Computer	Schmeltz, L. R.	TAB Books
Pocket Guide to Programming, A	Shelley, John	Addison-Wesley Publishing Co.
Practical Introduction to Computer Graphics, A	Angell, Ian O.	Halstead Press
Principles of Database Systems, 2d ed.	Ullman, Jeffrey	Computer Science Press
Programming Languages: A Grand Tour	Horowitz, Ellis	Computer Science Press
Programming in Pascal, rev. ed.	Grogono, Peter	Addison-Wesley Publishing Co.
Programming the IBM Personal Computer: BASIC	Graham, Neill	Holt, Rinehart & Winston
Proving Programs Correct	Anderson, R. B.	John Wiley & Sons
Run: Computer Education	Harper, Dennis O.	Brooks/Cole Publishing Co.
S-100 Bus Handbook, The	Bursky, Dave	Hayden Book Co.
Sargon: A Computer Chess Program	Spracklen, Dan and Kathe	Hayden Book Co.
Simple Guide to Home Computers, A	Ditles, Steve	A & W Publishers
Small Computer in Small Business, The	Smith, Brian R.	Stephen Greene Press
Small Computer Systems Handbook	Libes, Sol	Hayden Book Co.
Small Computers for Business and Industry	McKeone, Dermot	Renouf/USA
Small Computers for the Small Businessman	Libes, Sol	Dilithium Press
So You Are Thinking about a Small Business Computer	Canning, R., and Leeper, N.	Spectrum Books
Software Contracts	International Publications Service	International Publications Service
Software Handbook of Statistical Techniques	Alonso, J. R.	Sterling Swift

Title	Author	Publisher
Software Maintenance: The Problem and Its Solutions	Martin, James, and McClure, Carma	McGraw-Hill Book Co.
Software Metrics	Gilb, Tom	Winthrop Publishers
Software Portability	Brown, P. J., ed.	John Wiley & Sons
Software Proprietary Rights	Nycum, Susan	Reston Publishing Co.
Software Referral Catalog, 10th ed.	Engineering Systems Group	Digital Equipment Corporation
Software Reliability Guidebook	Glass, Robert L.	Prentice-Hall
Software Testing Techniques	Beizer, Boris	D-Van Nostrand Co.
Software Toolkit for Microcomputers	Schindler, Max, ed.	Hayden Book Co.
Some People Just Won't Believe a Computer	Spencer, Donald D.	Camelot Publishing Co.
Starting Forth	Forth, Inc., and Brodie, Leo	Prentice-Hall
Stimulating Simulations	Engel Enterprise, and Engel, C. W.	Hayden Book Co.
Structured COBOL: A Modern Approach	Mullish, Henry	Harper & Row, Publishers
Tales of the Marvelous Machine	Taylor, Robert and Green, Burchenal, eds.	Creative Computing
Taming Your Computer	Kanter, Jerome	Prentice-Hall
Techniques for Creating Golden Delicious Games for the Apple Computer	Franklin, Howard M., et al	John Wiley & Sons
Ten Easy Pieces: Creative Programming for Fun and Profit	Sagan, Hans, and Meyer, Carl D.	Addison-Wesley Publishing Co.
Understand Computers: What Managers and Users Need to Know	Walsh, Myles E.	John Wiley & Sons
Understanding Data Base Management	Freiling, Michael	Alfred Publishing Co.
Understanding Pascal	Ledin, George, Jr.,	Alfred Publishing Co.

Title	Author	Publisher
User's Guide to Home Computers, A	Eadie, Donald	Prentice-Hall
Using the Osborne 1 Computer	Lewis, T. G.	Reston Publishing Co.
VisiCalc DiskGuide	White, David	Osborne/McGraw-Hill
VisiCalc Home and Office Companion	Castlewitz, Davie, et al	MTI Teleprograms, Inc.
What to Do After You Hit Return, Or PCC's First Book of Games	Peoples Computer	Peoples Computer
What's Where in the Apple	Luebbert, William F.	Micro Ink
Will Someone Please Tell Me What an Apple Can Do	Polin, Glenn M., ed.	Sterling Swift
Word Processing: A Guide for Small Business	Smith, Brian, and Austin, Daniel	Greene
Word Processing Book, The	McWilliams, Peter A.	Ballantine Books
Word Processing Handbook, The	Stultz, Russel	Prentice Hall
Word Processing with Your Microcomputer	Schmeltz, L. R.	TAB Books
WordStar Made Easy	Ettlin, Walter E.	MTI Teleprograms, Inc.
Write, Edit and Print	McCunn, Donald	Design Enterprises
You Just Bought a Personal What?	Dwyer, Thomas, and Critchfield, M.	McGraw-Hill Book Co.
Your Career in Computer-Related Occupations	Koller, William	Arco Publishing Co.
Your First Computer	Zaks, Rodney	Sybex
Your IBM Personal Computer	Cortesi, Daniel E.	Holt, Rinehart & Winston

Manufacturers of Complete Microcomputer Systems

ALPS
190 West 800 North
Provo, UT 84601 (801) 375-0090

Access Matrix Corp.
2159 Bering Drive
San Jose, CA 95131 (408) 263-3660

Alpha Micro
17332 Van Karman
PO Box 18347
Irvine, CA 92714 (800) 854-8406

Altos Computer Systems
2641 Orchard Park Way
San Jose, CA 95134 (800) 538-7872

Apple Computer Inc.
20525 Mariani Avenue
Cupertino, CA 95014 (800) 538-9696

Atari
1265 Borregas Avenue
Sunnyvale, CA 94806 (800) 538-8543

BASIS Incorporated
5345 Scotts Valley Drive
Scotts Valley, CA 95066 (800) 222-0626

CIE Systems
2515 McCabe Way
Irvine, CA 92713 (714) 957-1112

CMC International
1720 130th Avenue NE
Bellevue, WA 98005 (206) 885-1600

COMPAQ Computer Corp.
12330 Perry Road
Houston, TX 77070 (800) 231-9966

CPT
PO Box 3900
Peoria, IL 61614 (800) 447-4700

California Computer Systems
250 Caribbean Drive
Sunnyvale, CA 94086 (408) 734-5811

Callan Data Systems
2645 Townsgate Road
Westlake Village, CA 91361 (805) 497-6837

Canon USA, Inc.
Systems Division
One Canon Plaza
Lake Success, NY 11042 (516) 488-6700

Casio, Inc.
15 Gardner Road
Fairfield, NJ 07006 (201) 575-7400

Challenge Systems
c/o Systems Sales
509 West 18th Street
Austin, TX 78701 (512) 476-7064

Coleco, Inc.
945 Asylum Avenue
West Hartford, CT 06105 (203) 725-6000

Colonial Data Services Corp.
105 Sanford Street
Hamden, CT 06514 (203) 288-2524

Columbia Data Products, Inc.
9150 Rumsey Road
Columbia, MD 21045 (301) 992-3400

Commodore Business Machines
Personal Systems Division
PO Box 500
Conshohocken, PA 19428 (215) 431-9100

Control Electronics, Inc.
707 Nicolet Avenue
Winter Park, FL 32789 (305) 628-3850

Convergent Technologies, Inc.
2500 Augustine Drive
Santa Clara, CA 95051 (408) 727-8830

Corona Data Systems
31324 Via Colinas
Westlake Village, CA 91361 (213) 991-1144

Corvus Systems
2029 O'Toole Avenue
San Jose, CA 95131 (408) 946-7700

Custom Computer Technology
1 Craftsman Court
Box 4160
Sedona, AZ 86340 (800) 222-8686

Data General
4400 Computer Drive
Westboro, MA 01580 (617) 366-8911

Digital Equipment Corp.
200 Baker Avenue
Concord, MA 01742 (800) 344-4825

Digital Microsystems
1755 Embarcadero
Oakland, CA 94606 (415) 532-3686

Dual Systems Corp.
2530 San Pablo Avenue
Berkeley, CA 94702 (415) 549-3854

Eagle Computers
983 University Avenue
Los Gatos, CA 95030 (800) 538-8157

Empirical Research Group, Inc.
PO Box 1176
Milton, WA 98354 (206) 631-4855

Epson America, Inc.
3415 Kashiwa Street
Torrance, CA 90505 (800) 421-5426

Franklin Computer Corp.
2138 Route 38
Cherry Hill, NJ 08002 (609) 482-5900

Gifford Computer Systems
1922 Republic Avenue
San Leandro, CA 94577 (415) 895-0798

Heath Company
see Zenith

Hewlett-Packard
19447 Pruneridge Avenue
Cupertino, CA 95014 (800) 547-3400

IBM
Armonk, NY (800) 447-4700

IMS International
2800 Lockheed Way
Carson City, NV 89701 (702) 883-7611

Instrumentation Laboratory, Inc.
Pixel Division
One Burrt Road
Andover, MA 01810 (617) 470-1790

Interactive Microware, Inc.
PO Box 771, Dept 3
State College, PA 16801 (814) 238-8294

Intertec Data Systems
2300 Broad River Road
Columbia, SC 29210 (803) 798-9100

Ithaca InterSystems
1650 Hanshaw Road
PO Box 91
Ithaca, NY 14850 (800) 847-2088

JC Systems
469 Valley Way
Milpitas, CA 95035 (408) 945-0318

Lanier Business Products, Inc.
1700 Chantilly Drive NE
Atlanta, GA 30324 (800) 241-1706

The Logical MicroComputer Co.
140 South Dearborn
Chicago, IL 60603 (312) 580-0250

Lomas Data Products, Inc.
66 Hopkinton Road
Westboro, MA 01581 (617) 366-6434

Magic Computer Company, Inc.
2 Executive Drive
Fort Lee, NJ 07024 (800) 221-1565

Microdata Corp.
PO Box 19501
Irvine, CA 92713 (714) 250-1000

Micromint, Inc.
561 Willow Avenue
Cedarhurst, NY 11516 (800) 645-3479

Molecular Computer
251 River Oaks Parkway
San Jose, CA 95134 (408) 262-2122

Morrow Designs
600 McCormick Street
San Leandro, CA 94577 (800) 521-3493

Multitech Electronics
195 West El Camino Real
Sunnyvale, CA 94086 (800) 538-1542

MuSYS Corp.
1752 Langley
Irvine, CA 92714 (800) 852-5362

NCR Corp.
Dayton, OH 45479 (513) 445-2075

NEC Home Electronics (USA), Inc.
1401 Estes Avenue
Elk Grove Village, IL 60007 (312) 228-5900

Netronics R & D Ltd.
333 Litchfield Road
New Milford, CT 06776 (800) 243-7428

North Star Computers, Inc.
14440 Catalina Street
San Leandro, CA 94577 (800) 447-4700

Onyx Systems, Inc.
25 East Trimble Road
San Jose, CA 95131 (408) 946-6330

Orange Micro, Inc.
1400 North Lakeview Avenue
Anaheim, CA 92807 (714) 779-2779

Otrona Advanced Systems Corp.
4725 Walnut Street
Boulder, CO 80301 (800) 525-7550

Panasonic Company
One Panasonic Way
Secaucus, NJ 07094 (201) 348-7000

Percom Data Corp.
11220 Pagemill Road
Dallas, TX 75243 (214) 340-5800

Plexus
2230 Martin Avenue
Santa Clara, CA 95050 (408) 988-1755

Quasar Data Products
10330 Bracksville Road
Cleveland, OH 44141

R. C. Electronics, Inc.
5386 Hollister Avenue
Santa Barbara, CA 93111 (805) 964-6708

RAIR, Ltd.
6–9 Upper St. Martins Lane
London WC2H 9EQ England

Radio Shack
1800 One Tandy Center
Fort Worth, TX 76102 (817) 390-3011

SDSystems
10111 Miller Road
Dallas, TX (214) 340-0303

Sage Computer Technology
4905 Energy Way
Reno, NV 89502 (702) 322-6868

Sanyo Business Systems Corp.
51 Joseph Street
Moonachie, NJ 07074 (201) 440-9300

Seequa Computer Corp.
209 West Street
Annapolis, MD 21401 (800) 638-6066

Seiko
c/o The Intech Group
2025 Royal Lane
Dallas, TX 75229 (800) 368-5010

Selectone Corp.
28301 Industrial Boulevard
Hayward, CA 94545 (415) 887-1950

Sierra Data Sciences
25700 First Street
Westlake, OH 44145 (216) 892-1800

Sinclair Research, Ltd.
2 Sinclair Plaza
Nashua, NH 03061 (800) 543-3000

Spectra Vision, Inc.
39 West 37th Street
New York, NY 10018 (212) 869-7911

Tecmar
PC Products Division
23600 Mercantile
Cleveland, OH 44122 (216) 349-0600

Teletek
4600 Pell Drive
Sacramento, CA 95838 (916) 920-4600

TeleVideo Systems, Inc.
1170 Morse Avenue
Sunnyvale, CA 94086 (800) 538-1780

Texas Instruments
Dept. 1A, Box 402430
Dallas, TX 75240 (800) 527-3500

Timex Computer Corp.
Middlebury, CT 06762 (203) 574-3331

Toshiba America, Inc.
Information Systems Div.
2441 Michell Drive
Tustin, CA 92680 (714) 730-5000

US Micro Sales
15392 Assembly Lane
Huntington Beach, CA 92649 (800) 854-8174

Vector Graphic, Inc.
500 North Ventu Park Road
Thousand Oaks, CA 91320 (805) 499-5831

Victor Technologies, Inc.
PO Box 9601
Mission Hills, CA 91346 (800) 842-9000

Visual Technology, Inc.
540 Main Street
Tewksbury, MA 01876 (617) 851-5000

Voyager Systems, Inc.
2192 Anchor Court
Newbury Park, CA 91320 (800) 235-3561

Wang Laboratories, Inc.
1 Industrial Avenue
Lowell, MA 01851 (800) 225-9264

Xerox
Office Products Div.
1341 West Mockingbird Lane
Dallas, TX 75247 (214) 689-6000

Zenith Data Systems
1000 Milwaukee Avenue
Glenview, IL 60025 (800) 447-4700

Zilog
315 Dell Avenue
Campbell, CA 95008 (800) 841-2255

Sources of Electronics and Computer Repair Training

Computer Repair Training Programs

Control Data Institute
HQC2AX, 81ØØ 34th Avenue South
Minneapolis, MN 5544Ø

Devry Institute, Bell & Howell, Inc.
Department 58Ø2, 22Ø1 West Howard Street
Evanston, IL 6Ø2Ø2

ITT Institute
35ØØ DePauw Boulevard, PO Box 68888
Indianapolis, IN 46268

National Education Corporation
Inquiry Department
4361 Birch Street
Newport Beach, CA 92663

Franchise Operations

ComputerLand Corporation
3Ø985 Santana Street
Hayward, CA 94544

Home Study Programs

Cleveland Institute of Electronics
1776 East 17th Street
Cleveland, OH 44114

National Technical Schools
4ØØØ South Figueroa Street
Los Angeles, CA 9ØØ37

NRI Schools
3939 Wisconsin Avenue
Washington, DC 2ØØ16

Manufacturers with Strong Technical Training Programs

Burroughs Corporation
Burroughs Place
Detroit, MI 48232

Digital Equipment Corporation
Field Service Group
146 Main Street
Maynard, MA Ø1754

Hewlett-Packard Corporation
3ØØØ Hanover Street
Palo Alto, CA 943Ø4

IBM Corporation
1133 Westchester Avenue
White Plains, NY 1Ø6Ø1

Radio Shack
5ØØ One Tandy Center
Fort Worth, TX 77251

Texas Instruments Corporation
Data Systems Group
PO Box 1444, MS/7781
Houston, TX 77251

Xerox Corporation
1341 West Mockingbird Lane
Dallas, TX 75247

Third Party Service Providers

RCA Data Services, Inc.
Building 2Ø4-2
Route 38
Cherry Hill, NJ Ø8ØØ2

Sorbus Service, Inc.
5Ø East Swedesford Road
Frazer, PA 19355

TRW
15 Law Drive
Fairfield, NJ Ø7ØØ6

Western Union Field Service Division
One Lake Street
Upper Saddle River, NJ Ø7458

Periodicals

ACM Computing Surveys: Quarterly. $40.00/year.
Published by Association for Computing Machinery, Inc.
11 W. 42nd Street
New York, NY 10036 (212) 869-7440

AEDS Journal: Quarterly. $25.00/year.
Published by Association for Educational Data Systems
1201 16th Street NW
Washington, DC 20036 (202) 293-7709

AEDS Monitor: Quarterly. $15.00/year.
Published by Association for Educational Data Systems
1201 16th Street NW
Washington, DC 20036 (202) 293-7709

Advanced Office Concepts: Monthly. $95.00/year.
Published by John A. Murphy
One Bala Plaza
Bala Cynwyd, PA 19004 (215) 667-5993

Anderson Report, The: Monthly. $125.00/year.
Published by Kenneth D. Anderson
PO Box 3616
Simi Valley, CA 93063 (805) 581-1184

Annals of the History of Computing: Quarterly. $25.00/year.
Published by American Federation of Information Processing Society
1815 N. Lynn Street, Suite 800
Arlington, VA 22209 (703) 764-9595

Attorneys Computer Report: Monthly. $89.00/year.
Published by Professional Publications, Inc.
PO Box 80280
Atlanta, GA 30366 (404) 455-7600

Auerbach Computer Technology Report: Monthly.
Published by Auerbach Publishers, Inc.
6560 N. Park Drive
Pennsauken, NJ 08109 (609) 622-2020

Auerbach Information Management Series: Bimonthly.
Published by Auerbach Publishers, Inc.
6560 N. Park Drive
Pennsauken, NJ 08109 (609) 662-2020

BYTE: Monthly. $21.00/year.
Published by McGraw-Hill, Inc.
70 Main Street
Peterborough, NH 03458 (603) 924-9281

Bank Automation Newsletter: Monthly. $56.00/year.
Published by Warren, Gorham & Lamont, Inc.
210 South Street
Boston, MA 02111 (617) 423-2020

Bank Systems and Equipment: Monthly. $30.00/year.
Published by M. Jeffrey Okon
1515 Broadway
New York, NY 10036 (212) 869-1300

Business Computer Systems: Monthly.
Published by S. Henry Sacks
221 Columbus Avenue
Boston, MA 02116 (617) 536-7780

Business Forms Reporter: Monthly. $24.00/year.
Published by Frank Veverka
401 N. Broad Street
Philadelphia, PA 19108 (215) 574-9600

Business Systems Update: Monthly. $39.00/year.
Published by PrimeStar Research, Inc.
701 E. Irving Park Road
Roselle, IL 60172 (800) 762-6800

CAD/CAM Technology: Quarterly. $36.00/year.
Published by Michael Jackcsy
One SME Drive, PO Box 930
Dearborn, MI 48128 (313) 271-1500

C B E M A Comment: 10 times/year.
Published by Computer & Business Equipment Manufacturer Association
311 First Street, Suite 500
Washington, DC 20001 (202) 737-8888

Calphad: Quarterly. $175.00/year.
Published by Pergamon Press
Maxwell House, Fairview Park
Elmsford, NY 10523 (914) 592-7700

Canadian Datasystems: Monthly. $19.00/year.
Published by Victor G. Zellermeyer
481 University Avenue
Toronto, Ont. M5W 1A7 (416) 596-5906

Chromasette Magazine: Monthly. $50.00/year.
Published by Cload Magazine, Inc.
PO Box 1448
Santa Barbara, CA 93102 (805) 962-6271

Classroom Computer News: Bimonthly. $16.00/year.
Published by Peter Dublin
Box 266
Cambridge, MA 02138 (617) 923-7707

Collegiate Microcomputer: Quarterly. $28.00/year
Published by Brian J. Winkel
Rose Hulman Institute of Technology
Terre Haute, IN (812) 877-1511

Commline: Bimonthly.
Published by Bill Gapp
241 Holbrook Drive
Wheeling, IL 60090 (312) 541-9084

Communications of the ACM: Monthly. $40.00/year.
Published by Association for Computing Machinery, Inc.
11 W. 42nd Street
New York, NY 10036 (212) 869-7440

Compensation Review: Quarterly. $28.25/year
Published by American Management Association, Inc.
135 W. 50th Street
New York, NY 10020 (212) 586-8100

Compute!: Monthly. $20.00/year.
Published by Small System Services, Inc.
PO Box 5406
Greensboro, NC 27403 (919) 275-9809

Computer: Monthly. $61.00/year.
Published by H. T. Seaborn
10662 Los Vaqueros Circle
Los Alamitos, CA 90720 (714) 821-8380

Computer Age: Monthly. $75.00/year.
Published by E. T. O'Connell, Jr.
7620 Little River Turnpike, Suite 414
Annadale, VA 22003 (703) 354-9400

Computer Aided Design Report: Monthly. $96.00/year
Published by L. Stephen Wolfe
711 Van Nuys Street
San Diego, CA 92109 (714) 488-2220

Computer and Communications Buyer: Monthly. $225.00/year.
26 Broadway
New York, NY 10004 (212) 943-9020

Computer and Information Systems Abstracts Journal: 12 times/year.
Published by Cambridge Scientific Abstracts
5161 River Road, Bldg. #60
Bethesda, MD 20816 (301) 951-1400

Computer and Programming: Bimonthly. $6.95/year.
Published by Davis Publications
380 Lexington Avenue
New York, NY 10017 (212) 949-9190

Computer BookBase: Monthly. $45.00/year.
Published by Interface Age
Box 1217
Cerritos, CA 90701 (213) 926-9540

Computer Business News: Weekly. $25.00/year.
Published by Patrick McGovern
375 Cochituate Road
Framingham, MA 01701 (617) 879-0700

ComputerData: Monthly. $25.00/year
Published by M. Summerfield
55 Bloor Street, W., Suite 1201
Toronto, Ont. M4W 3M1

Computer Decisions: Monthly. $28.00/year.
Published by Hayden Publishing Company
50 Essex Street
Rochelle Park, NJ 07662 (201) 843-0550

Computer Electronic Service News: Bimonthly.
Published by Wayne Green
PO Box 512
Peterborough, NH 03458 (603) 880-9171

Computer Farming Newsletter: Monthly. $33.00/year.
Published by Lloyd Dinkins
PO Box 22642
Memphis, TN 38122

Computer Graphics News: Bimonthly.
Published by Scherago Associates, Inc.
1515 Broadway
New York, NY 10016 (212) 730-1050

Computer Graphics World: Monthly. $30.00/year.
Published by Randall L. Stickrod
1714 Stockton Street
San Francisco, CA 94133 (415) 398-7151

Computer Languages: Quarterly. $135.00/year.
Published by Pergamon Press
Maxwell House, Fairview Park
Elmsford, NY 10523 (914) 592-7700

Computer Marketing Newsletter: Monthly. $96.00/year.
Published by Gerard Guyod
1000 Quail, Suite 120
Newport Beach, CA 92660 (714) 752-0271

Computer Marketing Opportunities: Monthly. $12.00/year.
Published by Gerard Guyod
1000 Quail, Suite 120
Newport Beach, CA 92660 (714) 752-0271

Computer Merchandising: Monthly.
Published by Bill Slapin
1570 Ventura Boulevard, Suite 610
Encino, CA 91436 (213) 995-0436

Computer Music Journal: Quarterly. $25.ØØ/year.
Published by MIT Press
28 Carleton Street
Cambridge, MA Ø2142 (617) 253-2889
Computer Retailing: Monthly. $4Ø.ØØ/year.
Published by W. R. C. Smith Publishing Co.
176Ø Peachtree Road
Atlanta, GA 3Ø357 (4Ø4) 874-4462
Computer Systems News: Biweekly. $15.ØØ/year.
Published by Thomas Cooper
111 East Shore Road
Manhasset, NY 11Ø3Ø (516) 365-46ØØ
Computers and Chemistry: Quarterly. $135.ØØ/year.
Published by Pergamon Press
Maxwell House, Fairview Park
Elmsford, NY 1Ø523 (914) 592-77ØØ
Computers and Education: Quarterly. $11Ø.ØØ/year.
Published by Pergamon Press
Maxwell House, Fairview Park
Elsmford, NY 1Ø523 (914) 592-77ØØ
Computers and Electrical Engineering: Quarterly. $17Ø.ØØ/year.
Published by Pergamon Press
Maxwell House, Fairview Park
Elmsford, NY 1Ø523 (914) 592-77ØØ
Computers and Electronics: Monthly. $15.97/year.
Published by Computers and Electronics
PO Box 2774
Boulder, CO 8Ø3Ø2
Computers & Fluids: Quarterly. $16Ø.ØØ/year.
Published by Pergamon Press
Maxwell House, Fairview Park
Elmsford, NY 1Ø523 (914) 592-77ØØ
Computers and Geosciences: Quarterly. $17Ø.ØØ/year.
Published by Pergamon Press
Maxwell House, Fairview Park
Elmsford, NY 1Ø523 (914) 592-77ØØ
Computer and Graphics: Quarterly. $17Ø.ØØ/year.
Published by Pergamon Press
Maxwell House, Fairview Park
Elmsford, NY 1Ø523 (914) 592-77ØØ
Computers and Industrial Engineering: Quarterly. $16Ø.ØØ/year.
Published by Pergamon Press
Maxwell House, Fairview Park
Elmsford, NY 1Ø523 (914) 592-77ØØ

Computers and Mathematics with Applications: Quarterly. $190.00/year.
Published by Pergamon Press
Maxwell House, Fairview Park
Elmsford, NY 10523 (914) 592-7700

Computers and Operations Research: Quarterly. $140.000/year.
Published by Pergamon Press
Maxwell House, Fairview Park
Elmsford, NY 10523 (914) 592-7700

Computers and People: Irregular. $14.50/year.
Published by Berkeley Enterprises, Inc.
815 Washington Street
Newtonville, MA 02160 (617) 332-5243

Computers and Structures: Bimonthly. $280.00/year.
Published by Pergamon Press
Maxwell House, Fairview Park
Elmsford, NY 10523 (914) 592-7700

Computers in Biology and Medicine: Quarterly. $140.00/year
Published by Pergamon Press
Maxwell House, Fairview Park
Elmsford, NY 10523 (914) 592-7700

Computers in Healthcare: Monthly. $12.00/year.
Published by Bill W. Childs
6430 South Yosemite
Englewood, CO 80111 (303) 694-1522

Computerworld: Weekly. $36.00/year.
Published by Patrick J. McGovern
375 Cochituate Road
Framingham, MA 01701 (617) 879-0700

Computerworld OA: 6 times/year. $44.00/year.
Published by Patrick J. McGovern
375 Cochituate Road
Framingham, MA 01701 (617) 879-0700

Computing Canada: Biweekly. $20.00/year.
Published by Paul Plesman
211 Consumers Road, Suite 302
Willowdale, Ont. M2J 4G8 (416) 497-9562

Computing Resources for the Professional: Bimonthly. $18.00/year.
Published by Computing Information Center
HG-45
Seattle, WA 98105 (206) 543-5970

Computing Reviews: Monthly. $50.00/year.
Published by Association for Computing Machinery, Inc.
11 W. 42nd Street
New York, NY 10036 (212) 869-7440

Control Engineering: Monthly. $40.00/year.
Published by Thomas H. Barry
1301 South Grove Avenue
Barrington, IL 60010 (312) 381-1840

CPA Computer Report: Monthly. $89.00/year.
Published by Professional Publications, Inc.
PO Box 80280
Atlanta, GA 30366 (404) 455-7600

CPA Marketing Report: Monthly. $84.00/year.
Published by Professional Publications, Inc.
PO Box 80280
Atlanta, GA 30366 (404) 455-7600

Creative Computing: Monthly. $24.97/year.
Published by Ahl Computing, Inc.
39 East Hanover Avenue
Morris Plains, NJ 07950 (800) 631-8112

Cybernetics and Systems: Quarterly. $384.00/year.
Published by William Begel
1025 Vermont Avenue NW
Washington, DC 20005 (202) 783-3958

Database: 4 times/year. $56.00/year.
Published by Jeffrey K. Pemberton
11 Tannery Lane
Weston, CT 06883 (203) 227-8466

Data Channels: Biweekly. $147.00/year.
Published by Thomas L. Phillips
7315 Wisconsin Avenue, #1200 N
Bethesda, MD 20814 (301) 986-0666

Data/Comm Industry Report: Monthly. $75.00/year.
Published by E. T. O'Connell, Jr.
7620 Little River Turnpike, Suite 414
Annandale, VA 22003 (703) 354-9400

Data Communications: Monthly. $24.00/year.
Published by George Werner
1221 Avenue of the Americas
New York, NY 10020 (212) 997-3139

Data Management: Monthly
Published by Edward J. Palmer
505 Busse Highway
Park Ridge, IL 60068 (312) 825-8124

Datamation: 13 times/year.
Published by James M. Morris
875 Third Avenue
New York, NY 10022 (212) 605-9400

Data Processing Digest: Monthly. $87.00/year.
Published by Data Processing Digest, Inc.
PO Box 1249
Los Angeles, CA 90028 (213) 851-3156

Data Sources: Quarterly. $60.00/year.
Published by Richard A. Norris
20 Brace Road, Suite 110
Cherry Hill, NJ 08034 (609) 429-2100

Desktop Computing: Monthly. $25.00/year.
Published by 10010001, Inc.
80 Pine Street
Peterborough, NH 03458 (603) 924-9471

Dr. Dobb's Journal: Monthly. $25.00/year.
Published by People's Computer Company
1263 El Camino Real, PO Box E
Menlo Park, CA 94025 (415) 323-9112

E D P Analyzer: Monthly. $66.00/year.
Published by Richard G. Canning
925 Anza Avenue
Vista, CA 92083 (714) 724-3233

E D P Industry Report: 24 times/year. $325.00/year.
Published by Patrick J. McGovern
5 Speen Street
Framingham, MA 01701 (617) 872-8200

E.D.P. Weekly: Weekly. $120.00/year.
Published by E. T. O'Connell, Jr.
7620 Little River Turnpike, Suite 414
Annandale, VA 22003 (703) 354-9400

EDPACS Newsletter: Monthly. $60.00/year.
Published by Harold Weiss
11250 Roger Bacon Drive, Suite 17
Reston, VA 22090 (703) 471-5751

E F T Report: Biweekly. $195.00/year.
Published by Sid Goldstern
51 E. 42nd Street
New York, NY 10017 (212) 599-2660

EFTS-Industry Report: Biweekly. $88.00/year.
Published by E. T. O'Connell, Jr.
7620 Little River Turnpike, Suite 414
Annandale, VA 22003 (703) 354-9400

80 Micro: Monthly. $25.00/year.
Published by Wayne Green
80 Pine Street
Peterborough, NH 03458 (603) 924-9471

Electronic Business: Monthly. $30.00/year.
Published by H. Victor Drumm
221 Columbus Avenue
Boston, MA 02116 (617) 536-7780

Global Electronic Information Newsletter: Monthly. $5.00/year.
Published by Pacific Studies Center
222-B View Street
Mountain View, CA 94041 (415) 969-1545

Government Data Systems: Bimonthly. $10.00/year.
Published by George Fine
475 Park Avenue South
New York, NY 10016 (212) 683-8430

IBM Journal of Research and Development: Bimonthly. $20.00/year.
Published by IBM Corp.
Old Orchard Road
Armonk, NY 10504 (914) 686-5688

ICP Interface Administration and Accounting: Quarterly.
Published by International Computer Programs, Inc.
PO Box 40946, 9000 Keystone Crossing
Indianapolis, IN 46240 (317) 844-7461

ICP Interface Banking Industry: Quarterly.
Published by International Computer Programs, Inc.
PO Box 40946, 9000 Keystone Crossing
Indianapolis, IN 46240 (317) 844-7461

ICP Interface Data Processing Management: Quarterly.
Published by International Computer Programs, Inc.
PO Box 40946, 9000 Keystone Crossing
Indianapolis, IN 46240 (317) 844-7461

ICP Interface Insurance Industry: Quarterly.
Published by International Computer Programs, Inc.
PO Box 40946, 9000 Keystone Crossing
Indianapolis, IN 46240 (317) 844-7461

ICP Interface Manufacturing and Engineering: Quarterly.
Published by International Computer Programs, Inc.
PO Box 40946, 9000 Keystone Crossing
Indianapolis, IN 46240 (317) 844-7461

ICP Software Business Review: Quarterly.
Published by International Computer Programs, Inc.
PO Box 40946, 9000 Keystone Crossing
Indianapolis, IN 46240 (317) 844-7461

IEEE Communications: Bimonthly. $15.00/year.
Published by IEEE
345 E. 47th Street
New York, NY 10017 (212) 705-7018

inCider: Monthly. $24.97/year.
Subscription Dept., PO Box 911
Farmingdale, NY 11737 (800) 258-5473

Inexpensive Business Systems: 4 times/year.
Published by Computer Faire
345 Swett Road
Woodside, CA 94062 (415) 851-7077

Information Systems News: Biweekly. $17.50/year.
Published by Thomas Cooper
111 East Shore Road
Manhasset, NY 11030 (516) 365-4600

Informatique Quebec: Monthly. $155.00/year.
Published by Pierre St. Arnaud
1057 Laurier West, Outremont
Montreal, Que. H2V 2L2 (514) 270-5481

Infosystems: Monthly. $50.00/year.
Published by John M. Luss
Hitchcock Building
Wheaton, IL 60187 (312) 665-1000

Infoworld: Weekly. $25.00/year.
Published by Infoworld
530 Lytton Avenue
Palo Alto, CA 94301 (415) 328-4602

Interface Age: Monthly. $18.00/year.
Published by McPheters, Wolfe & Jones
16704 Marquardt Avenue
Cerritos, CA 90701 (213) 926-9540

International Journal of Computer and Information Science: 6 times/year. $135.00/year.
Published by Plenum Publishing Corp.
233 Spring Street
New York, NY 10013 (212) 255-0713

International Journal of Policy Analysis and Information Systems: 4 times/year. $60.00/year.
Published by Plenum Publishing Corp.
233 Spring Street
New York, NY 10013 (212) 255-0713

Journal of Electronic Materials: 6 times/year. $125.00/year.
Published by Plenum Publishing Corp.
233 Spring Street
New York, NY 10013 (212) 255-0713

Journal of Systems and Software: Quarterly. $70.00/year
Published by Elsevier North Holland, Inc.
52 Vanderbilt Avenue
New York, NY 10017 (212) 867-9040

Journal of Telecommunications Networks: Quarterly. $100.00/year.
Published by Barbara Friedman
11 Taft Court
Rockville, MD 20850 (301) 251-9050

Journal of the Association for Computing Machinery: Quarterly. $40.00/year.
Published by Association for Computing Machinery, Inc.
11 W. 42nd Street
New York, NY 10036 (212) 869-7440

Lifelines/The Software Magazine: Monthly. $24.00/year.
Published by Lifelines Publishing Corp.
c/o Ms. Matthews, 1651 Third Avenue
New York, NY 10028 (212) 722-1700

LIST: Monthly. $23.10/year.
Published by Redgate Publishing Company
3381 Ocean Drive
Vero Beach, FL 39263 (305) 231-6904

LOCALNetter Newsletter: Monthly. $250.00/year.
Published by Kenneth J. Thurber
PO Box 24344
Minneapolis, MN 55424 (612) 935-2035

Micro: Monthly. $24.00/year.
Published by Mary Grace Smith
34 Chelmsford Street
Chelmsford, MA 01824 (617) 256-5515

Microcomputer Software Letter, The: Monthly. $125.00/year.
Published by Scarborough Systems, Inc.
610 Fifth Avenue, Suite 706
New York, NY 10020 (212) 765-3700

Microcomputing: Monthly. $25.00/year.
Published by Wayne Green, Inc.
80 Pine Street
Peterborough, NH 03458 (603) 924-9471

Minicomputer News: Biweekly. $9.00/year.
Published by Harold Buchbinder
1050 Commonwealth Avenue
Boston, MA 02215 (617) 232-5470

Mini-Micro Computer Report: Monthly. $75.00/year.
Published by E. T. O'Connell, Jr.
7620 Little River Turnpike, Suite 414
Annandale, VA 22003 (703) 354-9400

Mini-Micro Systems: Monthly. $45.00/year.
Published by Cahners Publishing Company
221 Columbus Avenue
Boston, MA 02116

Networks: Quarterly. $75.ØØ/year.
Published by John Wiley & Sons
6Ø5 Third Avenue
New York, NY 1ØØ16

Nibble: 8 times/year. $19.95/year.
Published by F. L. Mike Harvey
PO Box 325
Lincoln, MA Ø1773 (617) 259-971Ø

Office Systems Digest: Bimonthly.
Published by R. J. Whitsed
55 Bloor St., W
Toronto, Ont. M4W 3E2 (416) 967-62ØØ

Office Technology Management: Monthly. $79.ØØ/year.
Published by Joel S. Nadle
1ØØ76 Boca Entrada Boulevard
Boca Raton, FL 33433 (3Ø5) 483-26ØØ

On-line: Bimonthly. $78.ØØ/year.
Published by Jeffrey K. Pemberton
11 Tannery Lane
Weston, CT Ø6883 (2Ø3) 227-8466

PC: The Independent Guide to IBM PC: Monthly. $27.ØØ/year.
Published by David Bunnell
1528 Irving Street
San Francisco, CA 94122 (415) 753-8Ø88

P.C. User, The: Quarterly. $1Ø.ØØ/year.
Published by Jack Grenard
25875 Jefferson
Saint Clair Shores, MI 48Ø81 (313) 774-818Ø

Pattern Recognition: Bimonthly. $145.ØØ/year.
Published by Pergamon Press
Maxwell House, Fairview Park
Elmsford, NY 1Ø523 (914) 592-77ØØ

Peelings II: Monthly. $28.ØØ/year.
PO Box 188
Las Cruces, NM 88ØØ4

Peripherals Digest: Biweekly. $88.ØØ/year.
Published by E. T. O'Connell, Jr.
762Ø Little River Turnpike, Suite 414
Annandale, VA 22ØØ3 (7Ø3) 354-94ØØ

Personal Computing: Monthly. $18.ØØ/year.
Published by Hayden Publishing Company
5Ø Essex Street
Rochelle Park, NJ Ø7662

Pipes and Filters: 12 times/year. $24.ØØ/year.
Published by Walter Zinz
PO Box 5182
Walnut Creek, CA 94596 (415) 945-Ø448

Popular Computing: Quarterly. $8.50/year.
Published by Gordon Williamson & V. Londoner
70 Main Street
Peterborough, NH 03458 (603) 924-9281

Printout Newsletter: Monthly. $120.00/year.
Published by Datek of New England
PO Box 68
Newtonville, MA 02160 (617) 332-4576

Procurement Systems Digest: Monthly. $120.00/year.
Published by E. T. O'Connell, Jr.
7620 Little River Turnpike, Suite 414
Annandale, VA 22003 (703) 354-9400

Recreational Computing: Bimonthly. $12.00/year.
Published by People's Computer Company
1263 El Camino Real, PO Box E
Menlo Park, CA 94025 (415) 323-9112

REFERENCE: Bimonthly. $18.00/year.
PO Box 1200, Dept. D
Amherst, NH 03031 (603) 673-9544

Retail Technology: Quarterly.
Published by Ellis E. Rowland
125 Park Avenue
New York, NY 10022 (212) 371 9100

Selling Micros: Quarterly.
Published by Wayne Green
80 Pine Street
Peterborough, NH 03458 (603) 924-9471

Silicon Gulch Gazette: 4 times/year. $6.00/year.
Published by Computer Faire
345 Swett Road
Woodside, CA 94062 (415) 851-7077

Simulation: Monthly. $42.00/year.
Published by Charles A. Pratt
PO Box 2228
La Jolla, CA 92038 (714) 459-3888

Small Business Computers: 6 times/year. $12.00/year.
Published by Howard Falk
33 Watchung Plaza
Montclair, NJ 07042 (201) 746-4266

Small Systems World: Monthly. $15.00/year.
Published by Clint Baker
950 Lee Street
Des Plaines, IL 60016 (312) 296-0770

Softalk for the IBM PC: Monthly.
Published by Al Tommervik
11021 Magnolia Boulevard
North Hollywood, CA 91601 (213) 980-5074

Software: Monthly. $36.00/year.
Published by Thomas H. Politowski
PO Box 8359
Newport Beach, CA 92660 (714) 975-1215

Software Digest: Biweekly. $88.00/year.
Published by E. T. O'Connell, Jr.
7620 Little River Turnpike, Suite 414
Annandale, VA 22003 (703) 354-9400

Software News: Monthly.
Published by William A. Gannon
5 Kane Industrial Drive
Hudson, MA 01749 (617) 562-9308

System User: Monthly. $12.00/year.
Published by L. Thomas Caulfield
60 South Main
Janesville, WI 53545 (608) 413-4460

TI-MIX News: Monthly.
Published by Lark Doley
PO Box 2909, M/S 2200
Austin, TX 78769 (512) 250-7151

Teaching Electronics & Computing: 9 times/year. $12.00/year.
Published by Halvor Moorshead
Unite 6, 25 Overlea Boulevard
Toronto, Ont. M4H 1B1 (416) 423-3262

Trade-A-Computer: Monthly. $10.00/year.
Published by Philip Van Ostrander
PO Box 1173
North Miami Beach, FL 33160 (305) 462-4416

University Computer Centre Newsletter: Monthly.
Published by Dalhousie University
Computer Centre, Dalhousie University
Halifax, NS B3H 4H8 (902) 424-3472

Videodisc News: Monthly. $144.00/year.
Published by William H. Fields
PO Box 6302
Arlington, VA 22206 (703) 363-6392

Word Processing and Information Systems: 12 times/year. $16.00/year.
Published by Gerard P. McGowan
51 Madison Avenue
New York, NY 10010 (212) 689-4411

Software Houses

Accounts Payable R & D
8306 Wilshire Boulevard
Suite 50
Beverly Hills, CA 90211
(213) 703-0350

Ashton-Tate
10150 W. Jefferson Boulevard
Culver City, CA 90230
(213) 204-5570

Avalon Hill Microcomputer Games
A Division of the Avalon Hill Company
4517 Hartford Road
Baltimore, MD 21214
(301) 254-9200

Basic Business Computes
415 Cambridge Avenue, Suite 22
Palo Alto, CA 94306
(415) 326-0517
(415) 326-0775

Business & Professional Software
143 Binney Street
Cambridge, MA 02142
(617) 491-3377
(800) 342-5277 (Dial BPS)

Cload Magazine
PO Box 1
Santa Barbara, CA 93102
(805) 962-6271

CPMUG
1651 Third Avenue
New York, NY 10028
(212) 722-1700

CobraSoft, Inc.
13666 South Hawthorne Boulevard
Suite 5
Hawthorne, CA 90250
(213) 644-1135

Comprehensive Software
PO Box 90833
Los Angeles, CA 90009

Comprehensive Tax Systems
5707 Redwood Road
Oakland, CA 94619
(800) 227-2575

Computronics
50 N. Pascack Road
Spring Valley, NY 10977
(800) 431-2818

Continental Software
11223 S. Hindry Avenue
Los Angeles, CA 90045
(800) 421-3930

Creative Applications
2525 S. Wadsworth
Suite 206
Lakewood, CO 80227
(303) 985-4465

DAGAR
123 York Street, Suite 2H
New Haven, CT 06510
(203) 624-0500

E-Z Software
PO Box 591
Novato, CA 94948
(415) 388-0238

Educational Courseware
3 Nappa Lane
Westport, CT 06880
(203) 227-1438

Freeman Systems
7 Sunset Lane
Menlo Park, CA 94025
(415) 854-0457

Howard W. Sams & Co, Inc.
4300 W. 62nd Street
Indianapolis, IN 46268
(317) 298-5400

HumanSoft, Inc.
661 Massachusetts Avenue
Arlington, MA 02174
(617) 641-1880 0322
(617) 641-1881 0321

Instant Software, Inc.
Route 101
Peterborough, NH 03548
(603) 924-9471

John Wiley & Sons, Inc.
605 Third Avenue
New York, NY 10158
(212) 850-6520

K & S Systems
PO Box 634
Drexel Hill, PA 19026

Lexisoft
PO Box 267
Davis, CA 95616
(916) 758-3630

Lichen Software
6603 North Lee Street
Spokane, WA 99207

Lifetree Software
411 Pacific St
Suite 315
Monterey, CA 93940
(408) 373-4718

Magic Carpet Software
PO Box 35115
Phoenix, AZ 85069

Mark of the Unicorn, Inc.
PO Box 423
Arlington, MA 02174
(617) 489-1387

Matrix Software, Inc.
315 Marion Avenue
Big Rapids, MI 49307
(616) 796-2483

Micro Associates, Inc.
2300 Highway 365, LB 131
Nederland, TX 77627
(713) 724-6583

Micro Solutions, Inc.
8511 Washington Boulevard
Culver City, CA 90230
(213) 559-3940

MicroPro International Corporation
33 San Pablo Avenue
San Rafael, CA 94903
(415) 499-1200

Microsoft Consumer Products
400 108th Avenue NE
Suite 200
Bellevue, WA 98004
(206) 454-1315

Milton Bradley Company
443 Shaker Road
East Longmeadow, MA 01028
(413) 525-6411

Muse Software
347 N. Charles Street
Baltimore, MD 21201
(301) 659-7212

OASIS Systems
2765 Reynard Way
San Diego, CA 92103
(714) 291-9489

PC Software + ™
211 E. Dakota
PO Box 211
Spring Valley, IL 61362
(815) 663-8221

Peachtree Software, Inc.
3445 Peachtree Rd. NE
Atlanta, GA 30326
(800) 554-8900

Pearlsoft
PO Box 13850
Salem, OR 97309
(503) 363-8929

Perfect Software
1400 Shattuck Avenue
Berkeley, CA 94709
(415) 644-3644

Personal Software Co.
PO Box 776
Salt Lake City, UT 84110
(801) 277-3174

Prentice-Hall, Inc.
Englewood Cliffs, NJ 07632
(201) 592-2000 (gen'l #)
(201) 592-2490 (marketing)

Prosoft
PO Box 560, Dept. L
North Hollywood, CA 91603
(213) 764-3131

Quest Research, Inc.
PO Box 2553
Huntsville, AL 35804
(800) 558-8088

Relational Solutions, Inc.
8723 Woodleigh Drive
Houston, TX 77083
(713) 530-4161

Sensible Software, Inc.
6619 Perham Drive
West Bloomfield, MI 48033
(313) 399-8877

Sentient Software, Inc.
Box 4929
Aspen, CO 81612
(303) 925-9293

SimpleSoft, Inc.
480 Eagle Dr., Suite 101
Elk Grove, IL 60006
(312) 364-0752

Small Business Computer System, Inc.
4140 Greenwood
Lincoln, NE 68504
(402) 467-1878

Softstar, Inc.
13935 US 1, Juno Square
Juno Beach, FL 33408
(305) 627-5511

Sorcim Corporation
2310 Lundy Avenue
San Jose, CA 95131
(408) 942-1727

Strategic Simulations, Inc.
883 Stierlin Road, Bldg. A-200
Mountain View, CA 94043
(415) 964-1353

SuperSoft, Inc.
PO Box 1628
Champaign, IL 61820
(217) 359-2112

Tax Calc, Inc.
4210 W. Vickery
Fort Worth, TX 76107
(817) 738-3122

U.S. Robotics, Inc.
1123 W. Washington Blvd.
Chicago, IL 60607
(312) 733-0497

VisiCorp
2895 Zanker Road
San Jose, CA 95134
(408) 946-9000

XyQuest, Inc.
PO Box 372
Bedford, MA 01730
(617) 275-4439

Zenith Data Systems
1000 Milwaukee Avenue
Glenview, IL 60025
(616) 982-3592
(312) 391-8860 (marketing)